Live Laugh

Lemonade

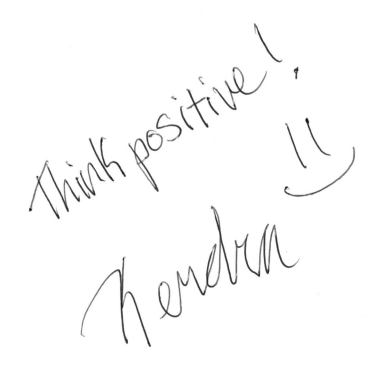

Think positive!

Kendra

Live Laugh Lemonade

A journey of choosing to beat the odds

Kendra Gottsleben

Dedication

This book is dedicated to each and every one of my family members and friends who have given me endless support and encouragement throughout my life – especially both of my parents. Without my parents inspiring me to never give up, I could never have achieved so many of my dreams and goals in life.

I also dedicate this book to children, adults, and their families dealing with life-threatening illnesses and/or disabilities. Obstacles are everywhere, that's a fact, but they should never limit you in life. Dreams and goals are attainable with hard work. It's been a passion of mine to help encourage others because that's what God would do. I have been blessed with so many wonderful people and experiences in life and believe that one should always be aware of those many blessings that one has been given.

To all my readers, please remember to keep moving forward, to never give up, and to make the BEST lemonade you possibly can out of the lemons that life gives you!

Contents

Foreword

I first met Kendra in the spring of 1985. She was five months old and I was in the fifth grade. Her mom, Betsy, was one of my coaches for Olympics of the Mind. I've always loved children, especially babies, and was at the age that I was eager to begin babysitting. I began watching Kendra for short amounts of time while Betsy ran errands and Dave, Kendra's dad, was at work. I imagine they felt more reassured leaving me alone with their precious little girl because my parents lived just down the street. I cherished spending time with Kendra! We always had so much fun together. I recall countless hours of building block towers so Kendra could knock them down. Wow, how she would belly laugh at that! I can still recite the first few pages of Dr. Seuss's ABC book from reading it numerous times. And of course, I still tease Kendra about the time that she threw up all over my favorite sweatshirt.

Looking back, I remember noticing Kendra's curved back as an infant and vaguely recall being shown exercises to help increase her flexibility when she was a toddler. None of it really meant much; to me, Kendra was perfect. I used to bike all over town showing her off to my family and friends. I conjured up any excuse I could to visit her and couldn't wait for my next time to watch her. Those times became fewer as I entered high school and tapered off completely when I went off to college. I still kept tabs on Kendra from a distance, but it was not the same.

In 1999, I moved back to Vermillion to teach and my relationship with Kendra was renewed. I was no longer just her babysitter; I was her friend, and part of her family. Kendra was in eighth grade, but had already gone through more than most adults do in a lifetime, as she will mention later on in the book. At the young age of fifteen, Kendra was more like an old soul. Surviving a near-fatal surgery gave her such a spiritual outlook on life. She was wise beyond her years. Her faith in God was so incredibly profound; it was almost as though she had a connection with Him that most of us never experience, at least here on Earth.

One of my most treasured memories with Kendra was her college graduation. I flew in to surprise her, but it turned out to be the other way around. When she walked across the stage to receive her diploma without assistance from anyone, I could not control my tears of joy! I had seen her walk short distances, but she spent the majority of her time in her wheelchair. I know her classmates and professors were shocked too.

Anyone who meets Kendra knows she has the kind of personality that draws you in. Her laughter is contagious and her spirit is uplifting. Kendra's motto is to make lemonade out of lemons, and she lives by it each and every day. Whether it's someone unnecessarily taking up a wheelchair accessible dressing room, a child pointing at her, or a waitress handing her a kid's menu at age 25, nothing bothers Kendra. She just shrugs her shoulders and keeps on going, making the best lemonade possible. Her resiliency is unending. It is with honor that I introduce her book to you.

- Jenny Chavers

Prologue

Ever since I was a young child, I have always loved writing about the exciting and troublesome experiences I have had throughout my life. I have dabbled in fictional stories, but those have never come very easy to me as a writer. However, one story I wrote as a young child that I am rather proud of was called "A Cure for Worry." The topic of the book was advising the main character, Mr. Ed, not to worry so much. This story was an assignment in seventh grade reading class where we were told to write a story based on one of Dr. Seuss's books. I decided to stem off of Dr. Seuss's book, "Green Eggs and Ham," illustrating and writing the entire book myself. Since that seventh grade assignment, I have continued writing about my own life experiences. I have always heard the saying "Write about what you know best," and I know myself and the incidents I have been through more than anyone else would, which is what inspired me to write a book about overcoming the struggles and challenges life has thrown my way.

I began writing this book a few months before I graduated from Augustana College in May of 2010. I was nearing the end of my college career and would soon begin the next chapter in my life. I decided to take on a longtime dream of mine—writing a book—and finally put it into action. I chose to take the leap of faith and take on the challenge of actually writing a book after a good friend of mine gave me the extra push I needed to start the writing process. With a long discussion and an outline of chapter topics, I found myself sitting at my computer and beginning to write just a few nights later. My wish for you, the reader, is that you also find someone who pushes you to obtain the aspirations you have only dreamt about in life. Surrounding myself with individuals who were as excited for me to write a book as I was to actually write it served as a great motivator to make my dream come true. Whenever I had previously thought about writing a book, I had always imagined that I would be older than 27 years old. Although I may only be in my late twenties, writing my story of overcoming obstacles just seems right for me at this point in my life. As I travel down life's path, I look forward to possibly writing another book. Who knows? Life is full of endless possibilities!

I chose to write this book not because I wanted to become famous or make a great deal of money, but rather to share my life's challenges with others and share how I stay positive with each and every challenge. Many people have told me that I have an amazing, upbeat attitude, even with all the barriers I have had to overcome throughout life, and that I need to tell my story of never giving up. I know how difficult life can be as a child, teenager, or young adult who has a medical condition or disability. If I can make an impact on even just one person's life, I would be honored. I have been tremendously fortunate in that, even though I have Mucopolysaccharidosis Type VI and am in a wheelchair, I have been able to have a pretty "normal" life (for the most part). I have always tried to live my life with a positive outlook, and with the notion that every hurdle I have to endure teaches me something about myself and what direction I need to take in my future. I have never wanted others to pity me for my struggles because I do not pity myself. Having a "pity party" for myself will never help me obtain all my ambitions in life. Everyone here on Earth has barriers to conquer no matter who we are, whether we are able-bodied or not, small or tall, young or old, rich or poor, bold or shy. I acknowledge that we do need to allow ourselves time where we just need to cry, scream, and get upset with some of those obstacles in life. But we must not dwell on them for too long because thinking about them too much does not aid us in reaching our individual goals and dreams. Life is full of ups and downs for us all; that is just the way it is no matter how we look at it. As long as we work through the ups and downs, we will be able to accomplish something great!

Imagine

Imagine talking to someone and not being able to look directly into their eyes.

Imagine people kneeling down while they are talking to you. Kneeling down is kind of them, but it can also be an awkward and uncomfortable situation for both of us.

Imagine wondering what classmates are thinking of you as they sit in class next to you.

Imagine trying to make friends when most people your age are unsure of how to act around you.

Imagine trying to be independent in everything you do in life, in a world that is not built for you, but rather taller people.

Imagine at times wanting to be "normal."

Imagine some people thinking that you will never be able to live on your own.

Imagine going to college where there are no other small people who you can talk with about life as a small person.

Imagine wondering one of life's many questions, "Who will marry me?"

Imagine wanting to do something that takes no time for a taller person, but for you it takes ten more steps before it gets done. Those ten steps are still the same whether the task is enjoyable or not.

Imagine feeling nervous around new people or the opposite sex who really don't know you or don't understand that you are not always shy.

Imagine wanting to show the world that no one can say or do anything that can hurt or break you.

Imagine even with all of these struggles, worries, and feelings that you are happy with your life and have accepted that "When life hands you a lemon, you squeeze it as hard as you can, add sugar, and make the **_BEST_** lemonade possible."

Imagine that you know that everyone has struggles, worries, and feelings of nervousness in their life, so you can't dwell on what you can't do or what you wish you could do. You need to take those experiences in life and use them to make the best out of what your future holds.

Written during my first year of college, fall of 2004

Chapter 1

*"To accomplish great things,
we must not only act, but also dream;
not only plan, but also believe."*
-Anatole France

How My Journey Began

Early Challenges

I am told November 3, 1984 was a beautiful, warm day. On this particular day, beaming from ear to ear, I graced my parents' lives with my loving presence. They felt blessed, as I was born healthy and strong at Sioux Valley Hospital (now Sanford Health) in Sioux Falls, South Dakota. I was so healthy, in fact, I weighed nine pounds and measured twenty-one and a half inches long. The doctors, nurses and my parents saw all of my potential in life from day one of meeting me. My day of birth gave no indication to doctors or my parents that my future was going to be any different from any other child. Little did my parents know, however, that this was only the beginning of seeing doctors on a regular basis.

When I was six months old, my mother noticed that I had a bump in the middle of my back. This concerned her, knowing that other children my age did not have the same bump. My parents decided to go to an orthopedist in Sioux Falls. The diagnosis was that I had a kyphosis, an abnormal curvature of the spine. The decision from that diagnosis was surgery at the age of thirteen months. As parents, they told me seeing their little baby girl being rolled away was heartbreaking and extremely scary. They had never pictured having to give their child to a team of doctors and nurses at such a young age. No parent ever imagines having to do that. Thankfully, the surgery was successful and my parents hoped that would be the only surgery in my lifetime.

Later, as I began walking, my mother observed that I walked with bent knees and that my fingers were rather short and curved. My parents made regular visits to the orthopedist for many years after my surgery. When my mother asked about my bent knees and stubby fingers, the orthopedist replied that some kids' knees and fingers are not straight and that it was not worth worrying about. The comments from the orthopedist did not calm my mother's fears; she was a teacher and knew that not all kids had those characteristics. She knew it was a sign of something wrong with my physical development.

At the age of four, the orthopedist realized that my mother was still extremely concerned with my bent knees and short, curved fingers, so he suggested that my parents take me to a local geneticist in my hometown of Vermillion, South Dakota. Based on the abnormalities in my stature and bone structure, the geneticist recommended doing a genetic test right away. Prior to the official diagnosis, my parents were told there was a good chance I would begin to regress intellectually and that I would probably die before I would reach the age of ten. The words from the geneticists were unimaginable and heartbreaking for my mother and father. My parents looked at me each day following the diagnosis, refusing to believe what they were told. They were trying to figure out how they would handle watching their child slowly die year-by-year in front of them. I was their one and only child, and the thought of me not being around was a challenge for them to comprehend. I was a very active, humorous, and fun-loving child. One evening my mother was crying in the living room while she watched me play with my Cabbage Patch dolls. When I saw her crying, I went over to her and said with a large smile and hug, "It is okay Mommy, everything will be all right!"

The month long wait for the official diagnosis was strenuous for my mother and father. They received the call from the geneticist and were informed that the unofficial diagnosis was wrong and I had been misdiagnosed. My official diagnosis was a rare disorder called Mucopolysaccharidosis, Type VI (MPS VI), also known as Maroteaux-Lamy. This new diagnosis would provide better odds for me to live a somewhat healthy life. I would not lose my mental ability, and there was also no age-related death sentence. The month of living with the first diagnosis was tremendously difficult for my parents, grandparents, aunts, and uncles. But apparently, even as a little child, I knew that God had a greater plan for me. I was not planning on leaving my parents and extended family any time soon. I still needed to make my impact here on Earth. The geneticist told my mother that it was estimated that about 1 in 215,000 births were affected with MPS VI worldwide. She also stated that roughly 1 in 25,000 births would result in some form of MPS in the United States. My parents wanted to know why I was affected with MPS VI. She explained I received this condition from the genes I inherited from both of them. Genes control all of our features, including our height and eye color, among other characteristics. Some genes that people inherit are considered "recessive." A special type of recessive gene causes MPS VI. The geneticist told them that when an individual who is an adult carries the abnormal gene and marries another carrier, there is a one in four chance with every pregnancy that the child will inherit the flawed gene from each parent and will be affected by the disease. Brothers and sisters who are unaffected by MPS VI have a two in three chance that they will be carriers of MPS VI.

In a "normal" body, mucopolysaccharides, or long chains of sugar molecules, are used in the building of connective tissues in a body. "Saccharide" is a common term for a sugar molecule, "poly" means many, and "muco" refers to the thick jelly-like consistency of the molecules. Typically everyone's body goes through a constant process of replacing used materials and breaking them down for removal. Children with Maroteaux-Lamy are missing the enzyme Arylsulfatase B, which is necessary for cutting up the mucopolysaccharides. The mucopolysaccharides that do not break down stay stored in cells in the body causing progressive damage. I compare the build-up in my body to a rubber cement like glue that builds up in my connective tissue and organs. My cells do not cleanse themselves, which causes the gluey like substance to build up and make my joints stiff.

Generally, babies show little sign of this disease right after they are born. When they do begin to show signs of the disease it is typically not until they are at least a year old. As children with MPS VI grow older, and more and more cells become damaged, symptoms begin to emerge. MPS VI presents a wide range of severities. It ranges from mild (someone only slightly affected physically and having to walk with a cane) to moderate (someone who needs to use a wheelchair but still has control of motor functions) to severe (someone who is strongly affected physically and has little control of motor functions). And at this point, my parents had no idea where I would end up in the range of severities.

After receiving the diagnosis, my parents learned that bent knees, short and curved fingers, and the kyphosis discovered as a baby were all characteristics of MPS VI. In fact, my surgery at thirteen months may not have even been necessary. When I was around five years old my mother and father were informed that I was going to probably have more surgeries and other challenges in the future, but that as long as I had regular doctor visits it would be manageable. They asked if there was a cure or treatment for my condition; there was not. However, one geneticist did discuss that research was being done on an enzyme replacement drug that could help me live a healthier and longer life. My mother inquired as to how long it would take for the enzyme replacement to be FDA approved. He had thought in the next ten years. My mother has since shared with me that, as she left that meeting, she left not believing I would ever receive an enzyme drug treatment during my lifetime. The geneticist also explained two other options were being researched – bone marrow transplants and gene therapy. Gene therapy was and still is in the experimental stage. My mother and father knew they did not want to try a bone marrow transplant because the procedure was enormously invasive and there was no guarantee of success. They thought that at that time in my life I was doing all right health-wise. Bone marrow transplants, in the experimental stage, were being used to treat very young children with Maroteaux-Lamy syndrome, but my parents thought that it would be the last resort in dealing with my condition.

Discovering Another Part of Myself

In the following years, the University of Minnesota Medical Center, Fairview and the doctors there became a large part of my life several times a year. The trips were filled with numerous cat scans, MRI (magnetic resonance imaging) scans, and lots of poking and prodding. I was never in the doctor's office when the discussion about my future or my condition took place. My parents never wanted me to see myself as being different from my friends at such a young age. They did not want my childhood innocence taken away too early. So, I would go and play with toys in the waiting area where my Grandma Drew usually waited for us, while my parents finished their conversations with the doctors.

I never realized that I had a disorder or that I was any different from my friends until I was about twelve. My parents and a geneticist we'll call Dr. "W" introduced me to MPS VI in his office at the University of Minnesota. I still did not grasp all of the information I was hearing at that time mostly due to the shock of learning I actually had a medical condition. I asked my mother, "So I actually have something?" To which she responded, "Yes, honey you do." I remarked, "I just thought I was short and had to go to doctors a lot." As a child, I had thought going to numerous doctors was a normal part of everyone's life. Even with that thinking, I do distinctly remember a time when I was seven wishing that my biggest worry would be learning my spelling words instead of anticipating my upcoming surgery.

My disorder has forced me to face a lot of challenges throughout life. I know God has given me these challenges for a reason. I have always tried to make the decision to cope with tough times by staying positive throughout the ups and downs of my disorder's symptoms. Many times as a teenager, I would say that it was like I had two lives – one life full of doctors, nurses, hospitals, surgeries, and pain, and a second life full of friends, family, laughing, smiling, and partaking in as many normal teenage activities as I could. No matter what, I know the future holds positive things for me, which is why I believe so strongly in making lemonade out of lemons.

Two Different Worlds
I am from two different worlds.
The first world involves the sterile stench
of hospitals, doctors, and nurses.
This world is filled with doctors treating me as if I
were a medical object and not a person.
This world is filled with knowing my health
is constantly in question.
This world is filled with yearning to simply be with my
friends worrying about the upcoming math test, rather
then being anxious about going into the OR.
This world is filled with countless life-
changing medical procedures.
This world is filled with having to have Faith
in the almighty power.

The second world involves being a "little person" in
a world built for taller individuals.
This world is filled with trying to prove to people that
I can do anything I set my mind to.
This world is filled with my desire for people to see
me as me and not see only my incapabilities.
This world is filled with amazing friends and family
that love me, because of who I am.
This world is filled with optimism, in that I can
make a difference in society.
This world is filled with understanding that God has
a plan for me and He created me just the
way He wanted me to be.

I am from two different worlds and I have accepted it!

Written in fall of 2009

Chapter 2

"Every great dream begins with a dreamer.
Always remember, you have within you the strength,
the patience, and the passion
to reach for the stars to change the world."
-Harriet Tubman

What Makes Up "Little" Old Me

Inspiration

Who inspires me? I am inspired by people who make the
decision to never give up on themselves or on what they want to
achieve during their lifetime. Inspiration to me is anyone who
ignores those who doubt and instead works to achieve their
personal dreams and goals. Many people may think I am talking
only about those who have a life-threatening condition, physical
disability, or learning disability, but I am talking about literally
anyone in society – big, small, tall, short, healthy or unhealthy.
One thing I find exceptionally inspirational is someone who is
wholeheartedly passionate about pursuing and reaching his or her
own dreams and goals. I admire people who have so much

motivation that it radiates from them, so much so that those around them cannot help but feel that same enthusiasm. I guess what truly inspires me are the people who are able to take the lemons life has given them and use them to make lemonade.

In June of 2009, I read the book *The Last Lecture* by Dr. Randy Pausch. While I did not have the privilege to meet him, his life and his works have been an inspiration to me. He was diagnosed with pancreatic cancer and was given only months to live. Rather than wallowing in his grief, he made it a personal mission to share his memories and wisdom with his family – and the rest of the world. Dr. Pausch inspired me because his view of life is very similar to mine. His notion about brick walls in life was dead on. He commented that the walls we hit in life make us who we are. They define us. The walls either keep us working toward our goal or cause us to give up. What I found most amazing was how Dr. Pausch was able to achieve all of his childhood dreams in one way or another. Some of his dreams turned out differently than he expected, but he was still happy with how each dream played out. There are not many people who can say they have achieved all of their childhood dreams.

Besides reaching his own dreams through his teaching, he helped others by enabling them to achieve their own individual dreams. He did not agree with other people who put limits on what a person could or could not do in life. He developed an environment filled with encouragement for one another, and stressed to all of his students that it was normal when pioneering new ideas there will always be arrows at your back. You just have to accept it. There will always be people who shoot down your ideas, but you just have to put up with them. His philosophy was that if one works hard for dreams, they can be reached in one way or another.

As I reflect on Dr. Pausch's belief that helping others adds fulfillment to one's life, I realize this is also a belief I value in my life. It can be assisting in a simple way or a sizeable way; it does not matter. Along with helping others, he talked about how loyalty is a two way street. He believed in Karma. When someone does well, then goodness will come the way of the giver. He wanted people to see that no one can get to where they want to be without others. The support from family, friends, co-workers, and students helps motivate a person in a healthy direction. I feel the same way. Dr. Pausch mentioned that we all need to find the best in everybody no matter how long it takes. I believe his outlook on life and people is what made him a great teacher. He showed the realness of life from his experiences. Dr. Pausch could have been mad at others because of all of the challenges he faced, but he chose instead to see all the goodness he had been given. A good teacher wants to see his or her students excel no matter what and a good teacher helps them along the way. That was what Dr. Pausch did and stood for. He passed on all of his knowledge of life experiences to be used by the students as a tool of dreaming big and working toward their goals.

After reading *The Last Lecture* I reflected on how I do not let other people or situations deter me from achieving my dreams and the goals I have set for myself. I have yet to share exactly what those ambitions are. As I think about my ambitions, each one usually falls within a few categories. The categories are helping people, designing clothes and shoes for little people, and being creative on my computer. The computer projects include creating slideshow movies, designing brochures, business cards, and advertisements for people.

My Goals in Life

My main goal in life and what I am most passionate about is helping families and children who have severe or life-threatening illnesses. I have been in the hospital many times and have had numerous doctor appointments, which helps me to recognize and comprehend what it is like to be a child with the medical world as an integral part of their lives. I know that I cannot relate to each and every child's individual situation, but I have a better knowledge than others do when it comes to worrisome doctor appointments. It can be an intensely scary time for children. Having someone who knows what it is like to want to be anywhere else but in the hospital or doctor's office can help to ease a child's fears. As I have grown up, I have seen how having a child with an illness can impact parents and the family unit. That is why I want to also assist parents through the process of dealing with severe illnesses and conditions. My family has been lucky to have wonderful individuals help us throughout my health issues, and I want to be there for other families during their challenging times.

My dream that coincides with this goal would be to work with children and their families with severe or life-threatening illnesses through the National MPS Society, Hide and Seek Foundation, Rare Disease Foundation, and/or any organization that has to do with helping children with illnesses or disabilities. My goal is to work with children and families at one of the local hospitals in my area, Sanford Children's Hospital. I have gone to the Sanford Specialty Clinic for my treatment for over nine years and feel at home with all of the doctors and nurses. I have been extremely blessed with such great doctors, nurses, and Child Life Specialists at Sanford Children's Hospital. It is a dream of mine to join their team and give back to others to make a difference in many children's and their families' lives.

Besides working closely with families and children, I would enjoy being able to use my creative skills within my place of employment. I have always been an artistic soul. I want to work on creative computer projects. Finding a job where these two criteria match up would be a job I would look forward to going to each and every day. I would be doing what I love and doing what I was put on this Earth to do.

Another aspect of my dream job involves a different type of design and creativity. For as long as I can remember, I have loved to put outfits together (and I have a pretty good knack for it). I would love to create designs for clothing and shoes that could be made available to individuals with short stature. I love designing and have designed my own dresses for my junior and senior high school prom. I have a passion for designing fashion for people with small stature...like me. Standing at only forty inches tall and being fashionable has given me challenges. My biggest challenge in trying to be as fashionable as my peers is finding clothing and shoes that are age-appropriate for me. There are plenty of items that are my size, but it is hard to find them without cartoon characters, pink flowers, or popular Disney princesses as part of the garment design. This predicament also goes with trying to find age-appropriate shoes. My dilemma with shoes is that my feet are very short and very wide, which makes it difficult to find shoes to fit my feet. As you can imagine, trying to find non-cartoon-decorated prom shoes was extremely tough. Thankfully, my Grandma Drew and I were able to design shoes to be worn for my junior and senior prom. I put my designing hat on with my grandma, and we came up with some pretty cute shoes. My grandma helped me not only with my shoes, but also by using her skills as an astonishing seamstress who was able to turn my designs into reality. She is also the woman who alters most of my garments. Rarely can I find something that fits me perfectly, and when I do it is nothing short of a miracle!

Finding fashionable shoes in my size is something I have always dreamt of, especially with high heels. Each fashion season that arrives with cute summer and winter high heels is disappointing because of the fact that they rarely come small enough for me. Recently, I did run across high heel shoes that were my size. While the color selection of the shoes I found was black, brown, and white, I still would love to be able to find some fun, colorful high heels like Jimmy Choo's in miniature form. The shoes I have are much more basic, but I still smile widely when I wear them because I finally feel like a grown up when I'm in them. While I wish it were easy to just *find* great shoes that fit me perfectly, I'm excited because it gives me even more of a reason to focus on creating a clothing line that offers fashionable clothes and shoes for little people. No matter what height a girl is, we all love shoes and clothes!

The passion for fashion is something I have always had, and hopefully someday I will be able to make my dream of designing a clothing and shoe line come true. The main reason I would love to see this dream come true is because I know that, no matter who anyone is in our society, people try to dress for success. As a person of short stature, dressing for success can be difficult. I know from experience at internships, conferences, and presentations that I have needed to dress for success numerous times, and it has usually been solely up to me to make sure it happens. I would love to help others in a similar situation as me to also dress for their own success. When individuals with short stature can put together an outfit that is not much different from fellow peers, it can make for a more confident person and creates fewer differences from the competitors or other job applicants. I have had numerous compliments on my outfits and shoes at various times and always get asked where I shop. I have had people comment that I dress up to date, but only in a miniature style. I always laugh and smile as I explain I buy my clothing and shoes where every other little girl shops that is about my size. I add that I am much pickier in my purchases than a typical girl my size. I realized a very long time ago that I was not going to be able to wear what others in my age group can, but I find some enjoyment trying to come up with somewhat similar looks and styles.

My dream of creating slideshow movies, brochures, business cards, and advertisements for others is probably seen more as a part time job or hobby. Over the past several years I have created slideshow movies for others that involve putting pictures in a certain sequence while music plays along with the pictures. Sometimes I have even placed actual movie footage amongst the pictures to add another element. Some of my creations have been for high school graduations, birthdays, weddings, anniversaries, Navy retirements, college athletic departments, and other such events. Also during those years I have produced brochures, business cards, and advertisements for family members and friends.

There is an amazing feeling of enthusiasm that builds up within me as I start out with nothing but a blank template and see where my creativity takes me. As for movies, I begin with nothing but a bunch of pictures, movie footage, music, and then end with a touching and beautiful final product. As for the other projects, I embark on combining words and various graphics to create an appealing outcome. I enjoy making the slideshow movies because I see this type of medium as a musical photo book. When music is added to pictures or movie footage it can hit a spot in someone's memory that has not been thought about in a very long time. I love seeing others' reactions as they watch what I have created for them. Many times I have as much fun making the slideshows as they have watching it. When I see tears swell up at the corner of people's eyes, I know that I have achieved a sense of happiness for them.

My Second Home

Since I am explaining who I am, I must talk about what my life is like at the hospital. Many people have asked me what the hospital is like. I usually smile and respond, "Well it's a hospital with all its ups and downs." The real truth is that, like everything in life, the hospital has its positives and negatives. The uplifting parts of the hospital are all the wonderful and caring doctors, nurses, and additional staff members who have come into my life due to my having MPS VI. There are many people I look forward to seeing each week when I receive my weekly treatments. There is never a day that I walk into the Sanford Children's Specialty Clinic without someone calling out my name to say "Hi." I know that I am extraordinarily fortunate to receive this fantastic treatment and I thank God for it every day!

Of course, as nice as the people at the hospital may be, the downside of a hospital is still the typical response when one thinks about a hospital. It is never enjoyable to be poked and prodded with needles. Life is full of circumstances that are not fun. But I try not to focus on the negative side of hospital visits. The fact of the matter is that the hospital has been a part of my life off and on for such a long time that it has become normal to me. I tell others that I am very lucky because I have not actually been in the hospital for long periods of time, as others have had to endure. In fact, November 2009 was the first time I had been admitted into the hospital for anything not related to MPS. I had pneumonia and was too sick to fight the virus with an oral antibiotic. The doctors wanted to attack the infection more aggressively with two antibiotics to kill the virus. Before that I had only been in the hospital for recovery after my surgeries. Even with that I have not had as many surgeries as many people think that I might have had. At this moment in my life I have only had seven surgeries. I know of many others who can double my number as far as surgeries go.

As a younger child I did not know that other people's lives had nothing to do with medical issues. But, I did find myself categorizing the two worlds that I felt I was in. I would comment that I had two different lives. One life is full of doctors, nurses, needles, and hospitals. The other side of life is full of friends, family, games, and laughter. Nevertheless, that was just a fact for me as a child and continues as an adult. Although I did not always see it growing up, I realize now that life has handed me a few lemons from time to time. When I think about all the tremendous people and experiences that have come into my life, I realize that I have simply chosen to use those lemons to make lemonade.

I AM

An M&M freak
Kendra E. Gottsleben
A retired dancer
A good friend
A person who loves dogs
A small girl that has problems like any teenager
A hard working student
A sixth grader at VMS
A person who loves to be with family and friends
I am the daughter of Betsy and Dave Gottsleben

Chapter 3

"The difference between the impossible and the possible lies in a person's determination."
-Tommy Lasorda

Parents that Never Give Up

Unconditional Love

Family is one of the most important things in my life. I have so many happy memories when I think about my family. My parents have been my number one supporters and have encouraged me throughout my journey in life. I know that I could not have become the individual I am today without their never-ending enthusiasm to tackle each dream and goal that I have set out for myself. It was instilled in me early that if I did anything, and did it with all my heart, I would succeed with my abilities. Giving my all was and still is a key to my life no matter how difficult or challenging my life is.

My parents have also provided me with an unbelievably strong faith-based environment that has helped me to overcome many of the challenges I face each year. I was always reminded that there was never a limit on what I could achieve in my life with God by my side. The feeling of accomplishment and satisfaction motivated me to continue to trust God and to keep going when I faced adversity. The continued support from my mother and father always being in the crowd cheering me on at every dance recital, music concert, and school event I participated in gave me the confidence to be the best I could be. It did not matter if work schedules had to be tweaked so that they could attend; they were always there. Even when I found myself doubting whether I would be able to achieve a certain dream or goal, my parents helped me quickly see otherwise and have continued to support me even now as I shoot for the stars.

Why "Can't" Isn't in My Dictionary

It was never acceptable to give in to the world's stereotypes, even though at times it would have been much easier for me. I distinctly remember my mother telling me at a very young age that the word "can't" was not to be a part of my vocabulary. She would say, "Kendra, you can say this is difficult, or challenging, or tough, but you saying 'I can't' is not acceptable." I had to at least make a valiant attempt at doing something before I could decide whether or not I was capable of doing it. She would always say that there were going to be times when it would be physically impossible to do certain things, but to not let that limit me. I learned at an early age that giving up on what I wanted to do would never get me anywhere. My father would tell me to be strong and that the pain of the sharp needles or the endless tests would soon be over. He encouraged me to keep thinking about the finish line, which for me was the end of a day full of visits with doctors. I still get a kick out of those memories of my father's advice, because he has been a college track coach for close to thirty years, and the term "finish line" came in handy with me even though I have never been one of his athletes.

When I was younger I did receive small rewards for being a good patient. I realized quickly that as long as I was a "good patient" with doctor appointments, needles, and MRI scans, the painful tests ended faster (which was usually even better than the fun treats I was given as a reward). More importantly, all of the medical procedures were bearable because of my parents saying, "We are here for you, and we love you no matter what! We are not going anywhere!"

School and Me

Even though I had a health condition, I lived a pretty "normal" childhood. I went from elementary school all the way through high school with my fellow peers. I was not in special education classes because my disability was physical, not intellectual. It also helped that my mother had an elementary special education degree. She had a lot to do with me not being placed in special education classes. Besides that, she had her master's degree in elementary education, so she was extremely familiar with the school system procedures and what is normally expected of children.

She always told me that all I needed were accommodations within the school system. Some of the accommodations I received included more time to take tests (due to my slower handwriting ability) and larger printed books (to compensate for visual difficulties). My mother was always extremely good at explaining to me when I was in elementary and middle school why I needed the assistance, and that my need for assistance did not mean I was much different from my peers. She helped me understand that the assistance I was receiving helped demonstrate my intelligence rather than holding me back due to my physical disabilities.

I attended St. Agnes School, a Catholic private elementary school where my mother was the principal. People joked with me in recent years that no one made fun of me because my mother was the principal, but I am not so sure that was the case, because for better or worse kids are kids. When given the chance, certain kids will always make fun of others. I have wondered if, because my school was a Catholic school, it helped my classmates understand and accept that God made me the way He wanted me to be. They saw me as their classmate – "Kendra just being Kendra." I also have another notion that the class I was in was an awesome group of students. We were all pretty close as classmates. We began school together in kindergarten and remained classmates all the way through fifth grade. I am lucky I began my education with that particular group of peers. It has been the key to my successes in life, because, besides a few different challenges, I was accepted as a "normal" fellow classmate.

While in grade school, I never felt different from my classmates other than just being shorter than some of them. For a while there were only two friends who were just a tiny bit taller than me, but not enough to really notice. But then, as children tend to do over the summers, my friends had a growth spurt before we started our fifth grade year. My first reaction was, "Wow, everyone besides me really grew a lot over the summer." My second thought was, "Now I can definitely say I am the shortest person in class." Besides being the shortest person in class there were some physical limitations that I had, but I never really thought much about them. I would say to myself, "Gosh, running and jumping really gets me tired, better go take a rest." Interestingly enough my grade school classmates never hassled me about those limitations and they easily could have. My classmates just seemed to accept that I was not as physically active during recess as they were, and seemed to think nothing else of it. Sometimes they would even give me their hand for support when it looked like I was getting tired of walking.

After completing fifth grade and leaving St. Agnes, my classmates and I had to integrate with public school students as sixth graders at Vermillion Middle School. I can truly say that I was nervous about the transition. I also know that I was not the only person who was worried. My parents were nervous too, especially my mother, as I would not be in her building if I needed her. I was mostly worried about meeting new people and wondered what the new kids would think of me.

Besides the change in school environment, I also had to adjust to sitting in a horrendously ugly, burnt orange chair on wheels as a result of my increasing loss of strength. My right hip was beginning to weaken and walking independently was tremendously difficult. Being in Vermillion Middle School required more walking down long hallways that were much further than St. Agnes School hallways. So, the Vermillion Public School system provided me with the helpful-but-unattractive orange chair. In order for me to get from one classroom to another, my classmates had to push the chair. My friends and I still make fun of that hideous chair. Besides the chair, I had to accept not being able to independently run around with my friends in the mornings before school started. I did not dwell on it, but those emotions would usually hit me shortly after one of my parents dropped me off at school for the day. Following each class throughout the school day, my friends and other classmates would argue over who was going to push me to my next class, which was always a pleasant surprise. This particular chair, as unsightly and uncomfortable as it was, also gave me the opportunity to meet many of the kids who were my new classmates. There were times when certain classmates, whom I never expected to volunteer, would push my chair to my next class or to an assembly. I ended up making many connections with my classmates as my middle school years went on, and that ugly burnt orange chair had quite a bit to do with it. Perhaps unseen forces placed that hideous chair into my life during my middle school years to assist me in breaking out of my shy shell and meeting new, accepting people. As I reflect now, the chair probably also helped my classmates see that being helpful is not too unpleasant and does not take much effort.

Even though my parents were afraid that the orange chair was an embarrassment, the truth is that it ended up becoming one of the best ways for me to make friends. I don't think I or my parents would have imagined in our wildest dreams that an ugly orange chair on wheels would have such a positive impact on my life.

My parents were usually pretty good at not showing how much they were actually concerned about my transition to middle school. But every once in a while I would receive unexpected visits from one of them. Normally the surprising visits were from my father, either because he was worried or because my mother had told him to go check on me over my lunch period. My mother's unexpected visits were normally when she would end up having a professional meeting at the middle school. As a typical middle school-aged girl, I was never very fond of seeing my father or my mother checking up on me. I still remember the first time my father showed up out of the blue during my lunch period. I was sitting at the end of the lunch room table with all my friends when one of my friends asked me, "Kendra, isn't that your dad?" To which I responded with an embarrassed look, "Yes, what is he doing here?" He made his way over to me, and I quickly questioned him as to why he was there. He explained that my mother wanted to make sure I was okay. I briskly clarified that I was fine and that he could go. I felt bad at the time because I was so rude to him, but at the same time I was overcome with embarrassment. As a new middle schooler, the last thing I wanted the new kids to see was Kendra's father coming to check up on her. After getting home from school that day, I kindly informed my mother and father that surprise visits during my lunch period were highly humiliating. If they were worried, they should make sure no one saw them checking up on me. I concluded with, "I am getting along just fine!" The surprise visits continued throughout my sixth grade year and then finally stopped. Both my parents realized that they were acting like "helicopter parents" by checking

up on me like that. Besides, they could see that I was actually
doing well in my new environment.

   As I have grown older I realize those visits happened only
because my parents wanted to make sure I was okay. The potential
for bullying and name calling is what probably concerned my
parents more than fearing I was struggling academically, but at the
time I think I was still (thankfully) oblivious to all the harsh
treatment that many middle schoolers could unleash at any given
moment and I didn't realize that was my parents' concern. I
believe my parents were torn between preparing me for what may
come and protecting me from the harsh reality of the real world.
They always reminded me that sometimes people stare and say
mean things to others and that I need not take what others say or do
to heart. The bottom line is that no parent wants to hear that their
child is being made fun of at school. The difficult issue is that, in
society, it really does not matter who anyone is or what anyone
looks like because bullying and name calling just happens. I am
one of the more fortunate individuals to be able to say that I was
never made fun of. Well, at least not that I was aware of.

   After my eighth grade year ended, it was time for me and
my parents to start thinking about my next transition in
life…Vermillion High School. My concerns about the transition to
high school had nothing to do with the kids. I had grown to know
my classmates very well over the last three years of middle school

and they knew me. The upperclassmen had seen me in middle school and were also familiar with me. At that point in my life I was more concerned with finding all my classrooms, making it to class on time, and successfully dealing with my challenging classes ahead.

As my mother and father had done with each previous year of school, we walked the route of my class schedule in order to see where each of my classes were in the building. Doing this always eased my nerves for my first day of school and allowed us to troubleshoot anything necessary. I was usually the only student who had a clue where to be, and I was always on time. This level of organization is a trait that I most likely inherited from my mother. Being overly organized is unusual for most middle school and high school students, but it has always been very beneficial for me. Even in college, I found my over-the-top organizational skills unique. For example, in my Education 110 class a student asked our professor, Dr. VanBockern, if he had brought a stapler to class for our papers. He responded that he had forgotten to grab his stapler off his desk before coming to class. I heard Dr. VanBockern's comment, and I chimed in that I had one in my bag of goodies that the student could use. After that student used my stapler, about seven other students came my direction also needing to use my stapler. Dr. VanBockern smiled as he commented, "Thanks, Kendra for being so darn organized!" I smirked at him saying, "No problem, I do what I can!" As he started collecting our class papers I thought to myself, "Thanks Mom!"

Transitioning to high school also provided a new and exciting opportunity for growth within my independence. My parents and I decided to purchase a motorized wheelchair. All through my middle school years, professionals mentioned to my parents that it might be good to look into a motorized wheelchair for me. My mother kept dragging her feet, but finally accepted that walking was too difficult for me. Just recently, my mother explained to me that the reason I did not get a wheelchair sooner was because she did not want to give in to the fact that my walking was not getting better. She told me that it was her fault that I had to use that hideous orange chair on wheels, and she was sorry she was so stubborn. I am not upset with her because during the time that we were completing the order for my wheelchair I was having mixed feelings myself. I was thrilled, but at the same time I was not sure if I actually wanted the wheelchair anymore. My concern was that I would be treated differently being in a wheelchair. I also felt that, by agreeing to get a wheelchair, I was saying to everyone that I was giving in to the notion that I would never walk again. Plus, I did not want to be known as "Kendra in the wheelchair." It does not make a lot of sense to me when I think about being in that ugly orange chair and never being made fun of but, at that moment in time, I could not help but feel the way I felt.

Fortunately, both my mother and I worked through our thoughts and feelings. Although I was not sure how exactly the change would feel, the day I got my wheelchair was unbelievable. It was my first step toward independence, and the freedom I felt was indescribable.

Unfortunately, my wheelchair did not come during the summer as I had hoped. I didn't receive it until school had already been in session for a month, so that meant the obnoxious orange chair followed me to high school. Finally the day came for me to get my wheelchair. After picking up my chair and being tested on my wheelchair driving ability (of course I was a pro and got the hang of driving it in about twenty minutes), I had a few hours of school left. When I got back to school, the students were all attending the homecoming assembly, and they noticed me as soon as I entered. There was no way to not be noticed. As it turned out, there was nothing to worry about. As the assembly ended, many of my classmates came over to look at my new set of wheels. Some of the guys even asked if I would let them drive it. I laughed at myself for worrying that people were going to treat me differently. This is just another example of things working out as long as you have faith.

Hello Oakland!

My parents have gone to great lengths to give me the best quality of life possible, so when I started losing ground physically during eighth grade and into ninth grade, my parents and I decided to submit my name and medical records to a research panel at Children's Hospital & Research Center Oakland in California. A few months later, during my freshman year of high school, my family received the call of a lifetime. It was November of 2000 and the call came from the Children's Hospital & Research Center Oakland. The Pediatric Research Center housed within the Children's Hospital & Research Center Oakland was starting a clinical enzyme trial. The enzyme they were going to study was the enzyme my body does not produce. The center wanted to know if I would fly to Oakland to try to get into phase I of the clinical enzyme trial study. They explained that I would have to go through a variety of tests before my family would know if I would qualify for the study.

My family left Vermillion around the middle of December, 2000 and flew to California. We were all very apprehensive as we sat in the airport waiting for the plane to arrive. I remember looking back as we walked through the gate door and seeing my Grandma Drew and Aunt Denise waving goodbye with tears streaming down their faces. I waved back, beginning to cry at the same time. As we finally lifted off from the Omaha, Nebraska airport, I wondered to myself, "Will I be an acceptable candidate for the clinical trial?" When we arrived at the Children's Hospital & Research Center Oakland, we visited with the head doctor, who we'll refer to as "Dr. H", of the enzyme study. He told me there were other kids with my same condition already in the study and living in the same apartment complex we were going to be living at. Dr. H shared that the parents and the kids in the study were really looking forward to meeting me. It was something I wanted to do and at the same time did not want to do. I had never met any other kids with MPS VI, the same disease I had. I wanted to see them because I wanted to learn how they have dealt with typical teenage issues and concerns that one has. I was also wondering if I would be able to make a good friend or multiple friends. The reason I was not ready to meet kids just like me was because of the unknowns of what to expect from the others. I was scared, nervous, and curious, but did not want to meet anyone right away. I was not ready to have my uniqueness seen in other kids' faces.

Two days after landing in Oakland, I found myself at the Children's Hospital & Research Center Oakland starting numerous tests, one right after another. I was poked, x-rayed, questioned, and examined. For one of my tests, I was asked to walk around a room for twelve minutes, as far and as long as I could without stopping. Another test was a three-minute stair-climbing test. Walking for twelve minutes and climbing stairs for three minutes straight were incredibly grueling tasks for me as my strength was extremely poor. They closely monitored my oxygen level and recovery time with each test. All of the tests were to determine if I would be accepted into the clinical trial. My mental state during the tests was to do anything and everything they needed me to do so that I would be accepted into the trial. I was pretty busy and tired during the first few days in Oakland with all the tests and doctor appointments, but when I was not being tested and exhausted, my parents and I enjoyed sightseeing in the San Francisco Bay area.

My family had been in Oakland for almost two weeks when the nurse, who we'll refer to as "Nurse J", working with the study, told me that the families were going to have a Christmas party. She thought it would be a great time for me to finally meet everyone. I looked at my mother with a slight smirk, hoping she would pick up on my hesitation to meet everyone. Of course, my mother ignored my signal and responded, "Oh, that would be great, we can meet everyone all at once. We would love to be there." Once again she was pushing me out of my comfort zone, as many mothers tend to do at times.

A day or so before Christmas, the day the families were having their Christmas party, I was free from tests. Since it was so close to the holidays, Dr. H gave me a few days off, so my mother, father, and I decided to go to San Francisco to see some more of the sights. My family left Pier 39 around 6:30 p.m. to head back to the apartment complex in Oakland. We thought we left plenty early to make the Christmas party that started at 7:30 p.m., but ran into a slight problem. We had forgotten that we were not in Vermillion, South Dakota anymore, where traffic is a little different than San Francisco, California. I didn't think the car would ever move, we sat, and sat, and sat. It took us thirty minutes to move an inch. From that point on we moved one block every twenty minutes. I was surprised because I actually was afraid we were not going to make the Christmas party, and up until that point I had not been sure if I even wanted to attend the party. One thing I was sure of was that I was nervous about meeting all the other kids.

As my nerves got worse and worse, we pulled into the apartment's parking lot, and went right into the party. As I entered the room I saw four kids looking straight at me. I could not believe what I was seeing; they really did look like me. The first question they asked me was, "Are you in the study, Kendra?" I told them that I did not know yet, and that my skin biopsy test was my next test the following morning. After that test they would let me know if I made it into the study.

I talked, ate, and played games with all of the kids I met. It was amazing to see that we had so many similar characteristics. Surprisingly or maybe not so surprising, the parents I watched helped their kids just like my parents helped me. As I looked at all the kids and their families I realized even more just how important the enzyme drug treatment was for us all to live longer and healthier lives. I also thought to myself for the first time, if I get into this clinical study, I will be contributing to the discovery of medicine for the future. I will become stronger, healthier, and as a side benefit, make great new friends from all parts of the United States and other countries. I thought about it and realized I already had great friends back home, but these new friends will know exactly how I feel and what my life is like dealing with MPS VI daily. There was an immediate connection with them.

As we were leaving, Nurse J stopped us and asked us to stop by her office before going to the skin biopsy appointment the next morning. I did not think anything of it, but I heard my mother and father asking each other why we would need to stop by Nurse J's office. They both came to the conclusion Dr. H just wanted to touch base with them about something minor. I had an uneasy feeling after watching my parent's reaction to her request. I went to bed hoping that my parents' reaction was wrong, and that everything would be okay. I hoped with all my heart to be accepted into the enzyme trial.

As we left the apartment, on our way to Nurse J's office, I got a funny feeling in my stomach. We were all a little quiet on the ride to the hospital. We entered her office and found Dr. H was already waiting for us. They told me I could go into another room and play on the computer. At that point I was extremely nervous. The whole time I was on the computer, I asked myself if I did something wrong. I also wondered if I had something else wrong with me. My last worry was the worst one – I was not going to make it into the enzyme clinical trial. I was on the computer for about an hour not knowing what was happening. Finally Nurse J came in and asked me to come back to the office. As I came into the room I knew something was wrong as my mother had been crying. We left the hospital and as we were leaving I asked my parents what was happening. They told me that I was not accepted into the clinical trial. The review board was concerned about a compression in my spinal cord and did not want to interfere with the possibility of delaying surgery. There are various types of compressions, and in my case this compression was a very abnormal and serious condition. It was caused from pressure on my spinal cord. Depending on the cause, severity, and location of the pressure on the spinal cord, the symptoms can range from temporary numbness to an extremity to permanent tetraplegia (paralysis of the arms, legs, and trunk of the body). In short, it meant I would have to wait.

I was devastated. I had met all the kids, and now, I had to leave and never see them again. I was also concerned that my health would continue to worsen. We were able to stay for a couple more days to say our goodbyes before we flew home. Our flight was not going to be a direct flight home. Our next destination was the University of Minnesota Medical Center,

Fairview, to talk to a neurosurgeon about surgery concerning my compression. As I was sitting on the plane, I did not really understand what was going on. I thought for sure I would get in the study. I asked myself why God would guide me to Oakland and then have me rejected. I asked that question over and over throughout the flight. The only answer I could come up with was that it was another obstacle I had to overcome.

After arriving at the University of Minnesota Medical Center, Fairview, we met with the neurosurgeon, who we'll call "Dr. L." Dr. L studied my MRI scan and told us we needed to schedule surgery to relieve my compression on C1 vertebrae. The surgery was scheduled for two weeks later. Being intubated was a four and a half hour process, but once I was under sedation, the surgery went as smoothly as we could have hoped. Dr. L told my parents he saw my spinal cord physically lift on the operating table, which was a positive sign for regaining my lost strength and physical abilities.

As I think about this adventure, I realize that God knew I needed the surgery at that time and made sure it would take place. This was a wake-up call from Him giving us the message as to what needed to be done first, before the trial. We thought it was the worst situation in the world to not be accepted into the clinical trial. We felt as though we were being teased, to have the enzyme so close, and then suddenly so far out of reach. As it turned out, it was the best-case scenario for me, because one year and one month later we received another call of a lifetime. It was Dr. H asking me to return to Oakland, California to be in phase II of the enzyme clinical research trial at Children's Hospital & Research Center Oakland. This time as a sophomore in high school I returned with regained strength from surgery and was the first patient accepted into phase II of the study. God truly works in mysterious ways.

As I think about the route it took for me to be accepted into the study, it is proof to me that God is continuously with me. I do not always realize how He is working in my life. The statement is true "Hindsight is always twenty-twenty." Although I may not have seen or understood the reason behind everything that happened, looking back I can see His guidance every day. My family had faith, trust, and hope in God, and so did I.

Graduation Day

Four years at Vermillion High School led to the incredibly awesome day of my high school graduation. I was extremely proud of myself, as were my parents. They had supported me throughout my entire life journey so far, and there are still plenty more years to go. The next life transition was one of the scariest ones yet – going to college. College was definitely scary, but not enough for me to decide to pass on the wonderful opportunity I had been given. In my opinion, college was the next step in life for me, no questions asked. Why would I skip college when absolutely nothing was holding me back? I had a solid GPA, excellent study skills, and an attitude to make a difference in the world. I was lucky because I had no pressure from my parents either way. I could choose to go to college or not. But they knew me pretty well – there was no way I would choose to not go to college.

I had been accepted to the University of South Dakota, South Dakota State University, Augustana College, and the University of Sioux Falls. From the time I was a child I had always thought I would attend college at the University of South Dakota (USD) since that was the university in my hometown. Being the daughter of a USD coach, and growing up with the Coyotes (the university's mascot), I had always dreamed of one day becoming a Coyote. USD was familiar to me, and as a child I saw all those "cool" college students and could not wait to become a Coyote.

These plans changed as a result of my parents' divorce during my junior year and my weekly infusions at Sanford Children's Specialty Clinic. I moved with my mother to Sioux Falls, South Dakota after I graduated from Vermillion High School. The move made my decision for me. I would be attending Augustana College. I chose Augustana College because of the accessibility and the stellar academic reputation.

My college career had its ups and downs in dealing with professors and classmates. A small number of professors and students saw my disability first and my ability second. As soon as I detected their misperception, I moved into top gear to change their perception, and in most cases I accomplished that goal. I focused on putting my intelligence to work and proving that I was as capable of achieving academic success as any other student at Augustana College. It did not take long for my professors to get the picture. I believe that challenging situations would have more than likely happened at any college I attended. It was an excellent learning experience. As I continue through life, I know I will run into similar situations from time to time. Thanks to my experiences, I now know how to handle them in the future. My parents, even though divorced, never lost sight of being encouraging and reassuring. Each one talked to me about the different college challenges, and they were angry that I had to experience them, but they also knew how much growth would result from my experiences. There were times when both my mother and father would ask me if I wanted one of them to talk to the professor I was having issues with. I would quickly respond with, "No way, that is the last thing I need – a parent defending me in college!" Each time I would say to my parents, "You have taught me to stand up for myself. I will get it taken care of. I just need some time to cool off." Usually after my comments, my parents, in a joking manner, would say, "Kendra! Welcome to the real world; you are becoming an adult."

Even with divorce as part of my life, I have never doubted that my parents cared for and loved me, and would do anything in their power for me. They have always balanced that with helping me realize that I have the ability to do anything I set my mind to. Nothing has been handed to me on a silver platter from my parents, and I appreciate that. If my mother and father had no expectations of me, gave me everything I wanted, and did not inspire me to reach for the stars, I would not have accomplished what I have. Having the ambition to write this book, and continuing to dream of new goals to reach would never have happened without encouragement and high expectations from my parents. Life is not easy, and I have been given the gift of knowing that confidence in myself is more important than trying to impress others. As long as I am happy with what I have achieved, then I know without a doubt my parents are proud of me. All parents want to see is that their children are happy, content, and confident to take on whatever the world throws at them.

In addition to transitioning to college, my mother and I moved from the only home I had ever known to a new city. On top of that, my mother and father for the first time would not live in the same town. I am, however, blessed to say that my father is in my life despite the hour-long drive between our cities. When his schedule allows for it, my father sits with me at my weekly infusions where I receive my enzyme treatment at the Sanford Children's Specialty Clinic. Having him with me at my infusions has been nice. Sometimes my infusions can get really boring with no one to talk to when I need to kill time. We catch up on what is going on in each other's lives and he fills me in on what is going on in Vermillion and at USD. Once my treatment is over, we typically end up sharing a dinner, which is always a welcome end to the day.

Through the many ups and downs of my life, I know I will always have the love and support of my parents. I am very fortunate for the family I have been blessed with. It's not always easy to see the best side of life when your circumstances aren't always ideal, but knowing you have the unconditional love of others to fall back on makes everything in life more bearable, and usually more enjoyable too. I am fortunate for the family I have been given!

Chapter 4

"Rejoice with your family
in the beautiful land of life!"
-Albert Einstein

The Importance of Extended Family

We Are Family

Having encouraging and devoted parents has been one of the most important factors leading to the unconditional support and love I have felt from them, but they are not the only ones who have been there for me throughout life. I have been incredibly blessed with amazing individuals that make up my extended family. With such compassionate grandparents, aunts, uncles, and cousins on both sides of my family, how could I go wrong? Ever since I was a young child, my entire family has continued to be unbelievably important to me. I also believe being an only child helped me build exceptionally close relationships with every family member. I have unique relationships and bonds with each grandparent, aunt, uncle, and cousin in my life.

Since the day I was born, I have felt an endless outpouring of love from my family. My Drew Grandparents, Gottsleben Grandparents, and my Godparents, Aunt Denise and Uncle Loren, came out to meet me the second day I was here on Earth. What has been so exceptional about both sides of my family is how I have always felt supported throughout life no matter where they live in the United States. Not all families are similar, just like not all humans are the same. My Gottsleben aunts and uncles have always lived far away, which has meant family gatherings are typically one or two times a year. However, many members on my Drew side live in the same state as each other, typically meaning holidays are packed with many family members under one roof.

I have so many fantastic memories of spending time with each set of grandparents. I have been tremendously blessed with the grandmas and grandpas I was given and, honestly, I was probably a little spoiled by all of them. But really, that is not my fault, for the simple fact that I was only a little girl. I did not realize until years later how spoiled I was. When I say spoiled, I mean in *all* aspects of my life. I received hundreds of hugs, kisses, chocolate chip cookies, cinnamon rolls, Dilly Bars, "Grandma-made" clothes, Barbie Dolls, tractor rides, Christmas lights on the patio (just for me), special Macaroni & Cheese, and mashed potatoes – the list could go on and on. However, all of this affection and spoiling never made me feel like I was better than anyone or more deserving than others; it simply made me see and feel the love my entire family had for me.

Tenderness of Grandmas

Throughout the years I could almost always be found in the kitchen with either of my grandmas. One of my favorite things to do with my Grandma Drew and Grandma Gottsleben was to assist with their baking. I was even given my own special apron for helping in each kitchen. Because I was usually the only grandchild at the Gottsleben household around Christmas time, I was the one who got to decorate the Christmas sugar cookies with frosting and sprinkles. I was also the chocolate chip cookie tester before anyone else was allowed to enjoy a cookie. It was a tough job, but someone had to do it! Grandma Gottsleben always gave me two cookies…one for each hand. At the Drew household I was the one licking the chocolate frosting from the spatula after Grandma Drew and I made Scotcheroos together. Sometimes, when Grandma Drew was not looking I could be found eating chocolate chip cookie dough right before it was scooped onto a baking sheet to be baked in the oven. Whenever my grandmas would allow me to lend a hand, I was eager and ready to help. Both of my grandmas have also taken turns in making themed decorative birthday cakes for me, such as a Mickey Mouse, Barbie, Carousel, and an M&M characters cake. In recent years I have not been able to give a hand as much, since my time spent with them is usually much shorter. I treasure the memories of those days. It is like they were just yesterday. There is nothing better than a homemade meal or cookie made by one of my grandmas.

Besides both of my grandmas being amazing cooks, they have always been very talented seamstresses. When I was young I could be found in dresses with many ruffles and polka dots. I was keen on them because I was definitely a girly girl. Even my socks had ruffles. I remember numerous times sitting next to both grandmas while they were sewing a dress with lots of frills. I enjoyed watching them take individual pieces of fabric and lace that looked like nothing, only to see them create a beautiful final product. As I grew into middle school age, I started disliking the ruffle and polka dot style of clothing. I still recollect the day I had to break the news to both grandmas that I did not want any more ruffles on my clothing or polka dot printed fabrics. After telling them, I thought that both Grandma Gottsleben and Grandma Drew took the news exceptionally well. As I look back on it, I think that my mother had a harder time adjusting to the switch than my grandmas did. It was a sign for the three of them that I was growing up and starting to make my own independent decisions. By observing my grandmas' creativity, I gained some of my love for design. I have been able to take my love for design in many different directions such as creating advertisements on the computer, producing slideshow movies, painting, drawing, and dreaming of creating a clothing and shoe line sometime in the future.

Both of my grandmas also added to my strong Catholic faith. I have always had so much admiration for them in their unshakeable and unconditional belief in God. I have several memories of explaining to both grandmas, at different times, how I was worried about upcoming surgeries or other events in my life, and they would encourage me to pray to God about it. They always stressed the importance of allowing God to help with our worries. He knows that life can be difficult, and I was advised to always call upon Him for His help. I was reminded that if I listened with my heart I would feel His presence. Many times I have said the Rosary with Grandma Drew during her scheduled adoration hour. Both grandmas instilled in me that, without God, we would be nowhere. We all need to take time to thank Him for all He has done for us…no matter how busy life becomes. A favorite scripture of both Grandma Gottsleben's and Grandma Drew's comes to mind, "I can do all things through Him who strengthens me" (Philippians 4:13).

Strength of Grandpas

Countless young children look forward to spending time with their grandparents – probably because they instinctively know their grandparents look forward to the "gift of spoiling." I have always been one of those grandchildren. Much like the special treatment I've received from my grandmas over the years, both grandpas have loved me and treated me like a little princess too. The memories I have with Grandpa Drew and Grandpa Gottsleben are very different because my grandpas (and the experiences I had with them) were very different from one another. Grandpa Drew came from an Irish heritage and was raised on a farm in Iowa. When he returned home after World War II, he began a successful farming career in northwest Iowa. As for my Grandpa Gottsleben, he came from a German heritage and was raised in South Dakota. He attended college at South Dakota State University, but was interrupted by World War II. When he returned after the war, he completed his education degree and began his teaching and coaching career in South Dakota. When he retired, he had served as Superintendent of Schools in the Lake Preston School District and, prior to that, the Montrose School District. There was, however, one common thread that both of my grandpas shared, and that was the unconditional love I felt from each of them throughout my life.

Grandpa Drew farmed until his early seventies, so many of my memories have to do with being on the farm. Although my Grandpa Drew recently passed away, my Grandma Drew still lives on their farm today. It truly was an incredible place to experience life as a growing child. I remember riding around in a big red International tractor with Grandpa as I honked the loud, low-pitched horn. Sometimes it was not only me riding in the tractor, but also my cousins, Sean and Patrick. We loved riding with Grandpa and waving at Grandma as she stood up by the house waving back. As my cousins and I grew up and started reaching the age where Grandpa allowed us to drive the lawn mower, you could find us buzzing around the farm while Grandpa worked in the machine shed tinkering on some tractor part. I have a vivid memory of my cousins Amanda and Sean and I riding the lawn mower and nearly crashing into the chicken coop. We never shared that story with Grandpa, but looking back on it, I bet he probably would've just laughed about it. As grandchildren, we had our moments of wildness. I believe that was partly why Grandpa rarely asked us to actually mow the lawn. Besides, Grandpa had a certain way he liked his lawn to look when it was done, and our antics weren't the best way to get it done "right."

As I grew older, my relationship with my grandpa continued to grow too. I loved listening to his stories about being in the army, what life was like in his day, and when he met Grandma. When he told about his war stories, sometimes he even brought out his souvenirs and pictures he had kept from World War II. Even though Grandpa never had to fight overseas, I was always very proud of him. He was an airplane mechanic that worked on B-26's while in the army. Not only was he mechanically inclined when it came to airplanes, but he also used his skills on tractors and farm equipment. After being honorably discharged from the army, his next career was farming. I always loved his stories about farming before all of the modern technology of today. It completely makes sense to me why, at times, my family would find him sitting outside in silence admiring his farm. He put a tremendous amount of work into his farm and never came close to losing it when so many farmers in his community did lose their land.

Over the years, Grandpa and I enjoyed more than a few good games of dominos at the kitchen table. When he first began teaching me to play, I know he was letting me win, as many grandpas would. I finally had to inform him that he needed to play the game for real, and if I lost, then I lost. He chuckled at me and agreed. Although I did lose a few times right away, I eventually improved and finally started to win all on my own. As we played, he usually would relay stories of his childhood to me. He shared how he did chores as a young boy, how he would walk a mile to his one room country school, and how they used horses in the field to get the ground ready for planting. Smiling and listening to his many stories was without a doubt the highlight of all the time I spent with him.

Unfortunately, I will never hear those amazing stories again as Grandpa Drew unexpectedly passed away on October 24, 2010 from a stroke. The last time I saw him I gave him an extremely

huge hug and followed it up with a kiss on his cheek, and he did
the same to me. We always hugged and kissed each other when
one of us was leaving to head home, but I had a sudden urge to
give a longer and larger hug than usual that last time. Now, I am
so thankful that I did so. We both were given the opportunity to
convey our love for each other and we both took it. The loss of my
Grandpa Drew has been unbelievably difficult to get through, but I
know he is in an extremely beautiful place with God and I know he
wants me to remember the happy memories we shared together
much more than dwelling on his absence.

As for my memories with Grandpa Gottsleben, they almost
always had to do with sports-related events, as sports were a
passion we both shared. Many times, my Gottsleben grandparents,
my father, and I would travel to Minneapolis, Minnesota to watch
the Minnesota Twins play. Grandpa Gottsleben and I both enjoyed
watching Kirby Puckett in action. When his name was yelled
throughout the Twins stadium, we quickly began cheering him on.
I also have numerous memories of watching the Twins in the
Gottsleben household on television. Another sports-filled memory
is watching the University of South Dakota Track and Field team
from the sidelines. My grandpa and I both shared in being
extremely proud of the USD Track and Field coach, because it was
his son and my father. My father even gave Grandpa and me
matching USD Track and Field jackets, just like the athletes wore.

We both thought that it was pretty darn cool. The ironic note is that both my father and Grandpa Gottsleben ran track for South Dakota State University – USD's number one rival.

A Christmas tradition I looked forward to as a child was Grandpa driving us around Brookings, South Dakota, to look at neighborhoods of lights gleaming and blinking everywhere. Knowing how much I enjoyed the Christmas Season, Grandpa would decorate the patio with beautiful colored lights and other Christmas décor just for me. Another custom at the Gottsleben household was our Christmas Eve fondue. Grandpa Gottsleben always requested to have either the blue or yellow fondue fork, because those were the colors of the college he graduated from - South Dakota State University. He was a Jackrabbit at heart. Even though he was a Jackrabbit, he still cheered for the rival Coyote track team at USD (when they were not competing against SDSU of course).

I have countless memories of coming around the corner and finding Grandpa sitting in his special spot in the kitchen with his newspaper in hand, a cup of coffee on the table cooling while he listened to a Twins game on his radio. Sometimes I could find him listening to his radio out on the patio as he admired the beautiful flowers and tomatoes he had planted. Still to this day I cannot pass by Juicy Fruit gum in the store without thinking about Grandpa Gottsleben. He always had a pack wherever he was.

Sadly, Grandpa Gottsleben passed away on December 3, 2008 from pneumonia. I will never forget the last day I spoke with him because we both got the chance to tell one another that we loved each other. Interestingly, we stayed on the phone with each other that day longer then we typically ever did. We discussed my college classes and other life goals I had, and revisited a few of our favorite stories and memories. Losing him was a challenge to get through, but what helped me was knowing that, just like my Grandpa Drew, my Grandpa Gottsleben and I were both given the chance to express our love to each other, and we both took it. Grandpa Gottsleben has been walking hand in hand with God, and it seems like every day I remember a fond memory that we shared together during my lifetime.

Aunts, Uncles, and Cousins

Besides having awesome grandparents, I have some pretty amazing aunts, uncles, and cousins on both sides of my family. I am not sure I could have asked for better relatives. I enjoy every minute I am able to spend time with all of my family members. With the modern day technology of e-mail, cell phones, texting, Facebook, and Skype, I have the ability to send and receive support through many different avenues, and this technology keeps me in touch with my relatives who are farthest away. One example of how e-mail has assisted me in writing this book is sending chapter by chapter to my Aunt Mary, who happens to be a high school English teacher in Oklahoma. Skype has also made it possible for me to visit with my relatives from Maryland, Japan, and Florida also. Using picture texting, my cousin Amanda and her husband are able to send frequent picture updates of their daughter Avery. Amanda is so proud of her little girl and wants her to know what it is like to know her extended family, but because they live in eastern Iowa it is difficult to see each other as often as we would like. Facebook is one of my favorite ways to communicate with most of my cousins on both sides. Since growing up and starting our individual lives, my cousins are spread throughout the United States. I am able to see what my cousin Patrick is up to while he is serving our country in the United States Navy. I am also able to see pictures and movies of my cousin Laura and her husband's little one, Bishop, as he grows into a young man. I am able to feel as though I have a close connection even though she lives in California.

From an outsider's point of view, my Drew family gatherings could be overwhelming as we are all trying to talk with each other at the same time. That may have to do with the fact that my mother is one of five children. For some holidays there can be up to twenty-two or more in attendance. There is never a dull moment when we are all with one another. There are jokes and laughter heard throughout the entire time we're together. I have many wonderful memories of holidays spent around the dining room table. One time my mother, her sisters, and her brothers told stories about climbing to the top of the barn loft and swinging from the top to the floor on a rope. As they relayed the stories Grandma Drew made comments about how unsafe that was. She also added that it was good she never found out about it or they would have all been in big trouble.

On the other hand, the Gottsleben gatherings are full of conversations where we each take turns sharing and listening to the stories and memories. My father is one of three children and each child lives in a different state, so the crowd of individuals being able to gather together is challenging, especially now with the grandchildren also spread throughout in the United States. When I was younger, and we were all able to get together in the summer, we had numerous conversations on the patio surrounded by Grandpa Gottsleben's beautiful flowers. I remember great memories of spending the Fourth of July on blankets in the park watching the parade in the afternoon, and looking forward to the bright colored fireworks exploding in the warm night air. Summer was the time when it was easier for all of us to see one another, because none of us had to fight weather conditions.

A Source of Strength

Family is one of the most important parts of life, and I am an extremely lucky person to have such great relatives in my life who care so much for me. I realize that not everyone has that gift.

I have never taken my large, supportive family for granted. I cannot recall a time in my life that there has not been at least three or four family members that have come through for me when I have needed someone with me at a critical time in my life. What makes my family so inspiring is that it does not matter who is having the big event in their life – we are all present if we are able. If we are unable to attend, we make it a point to let them know that we are thinking about them and are extremely proud of them. My extended family supports each and every one in all they do. I cannot imagine my life without my family. They mean the world to me! I would say that my family is where I gain the strength to never give up on my hopes and dreams for my future. They are always there cheering me on no matter how tough the battle has been.

- MEMORIES -

I am one of the lucky people on this Earth to say that BJ
Gottsleben was in my life.

I am even luckier because I can say that BJ Gottsleben
is my Grandpa.

I have so many wonderful memories of Grandpa in my life…

Memories of Grandpa loving the Minnesota Twins baseball team
and watching them on television.

Memories of seeing the Twins with him, as we sat there cheering
for Kirby Puckett.

Memories of sitting out on the patio during the summer admiring
Grandpa's beautiful flowers.

Memories of Grandpa putting Christmas lights up on the patio just
because I loved Christmas lights.

Memories of Christmas Eve fonduing and Grandpa having to have
the yellow or blue fondue stick, because those are SDSU colors.

Memories of Grandpa driving us around looking at Christmas
lights in Brookings.

The memory of having a matching USD Track and Field coat
with my Grandpa.

The memory of asking Grandpa for a row row, when I was five,
and him not having a clue what I wanted.

Memories of Grandpa sitting in the kitchen in his special corner
with his newspaper, cup of coffee, and his radio.

Memories of Grandpa chewing his yellow Juicy Fruit gum.

Memories of Grandpa asking me about school and my life.

Memories of Grandpa in my hospital rooms, sitting quietly and being there to support me.

Memories of Grandpa loving to give my dad a hard time about how the Jacks were doing better than the Coyotes.

Memories of Grandpa loving to golf with my dad and my Aunt Sheila.

The memory of Grandpa telling me that I sang well at one of my Augustana Women's Choir concerts.

The memory of telling Grandpa that I loved him on Thanksgiving Day for the last time.

The memory of Grandpa telling me that he loved me on Thanksgiving Day for the last time.

I may have lost my Grandpa Gottsleben here on Earth, but I have gained him as an Angel in Heaven to watch over and protect me.

I may not be able to physically see him, but he is there all around me and everyone he loved in his life.

I am lucky because I know BJ Gottsleben loved me and I am his granddaughter.

Written the day before Grandpa Gottsleben's wake, December 2008

- GRANDPA YOU WERE THERE -

I have been extremely blessed to say that Maurice Drew
was in my life.

I am even more fortunate because I am able to say that Maurice
Drew is my Grandpa.

I have so many amazing memories of Grandpa being there...

You were there shortly after my birth in November of 1984.

You were there giving me nicknames of "Niddy Noddy"
and "Sober Socks," as you held me in your strong and
ever so secure arms.

You were there spoiling me with hugs, kisses, and unconditional
love no matter what.

You were there in the crowd for all music concerts and dance
recitals cheering me on.

You were there when I needed prayers, as I would lie in the
hospital and throughout my life.

You were there to celebrate all birthdays, weddings, and holidays.

You were there giving tractor rides to grandchildren, putting air
in my wheelchair tires, and playing dominos at the
kitchen table with me.

You were there singing along with me on the lengthy car rides, as
we traveled across Iowa to visit Amanda and Isaac.

You were there sharing stories about your upbringing, years in the
Army, meeting Grandma Drew for the first time, and funny little
anecdotes that had a clean version and a colorful one.

You were there to fix anything and everything that was broken
down, short-circuited, or needed sprucing up.

You were there always smiling and laughing as we caught
bullheads, had weenie roasts, roasted marshmallows and sat
around the fire pit and reminisced.

You were there for advice and always when someone needed
a listening ear.

You were there for Grandma, your five children, seven
grandchildren, four great-grandchildren, other family members
and friends when someone was in need.

You may not be here physically on Earth anymore, but I realize
I have gained you as an Angel in Heaven to watch
over and protect me.

Your presence is felt each and every day and will never be truly
gone for everyone you have ever loved in your life.

I am fortunate because I know Maurice Drew has always loved me
and that I am one of his three granddaughters.

I will never forget you Grandpa and you will be forever in my
heart---I LOVE YOU!!!

Written two days before Grandpa Drew's wake, October 2010

Chapter 5

"Friendship with one's self is important,
because without it,
one cannot be friends with anyone else."
-Eleanor Roosevelt

Bonds of Friendship

Early Friendships

Throughout my life I have been blessed with amazing friends. Although friends tend to grow apart as they get older, I have always remained close to many of my elementary and high school friends, and those friendships have helped motivate me to always make lemonade whenever life hands me lemons. To say that they have inspired me and encouraged me over the years would be an understatement.

In the early years of elementary school I mostly played house, dolls, restaurant, and hung out with friends during our recesses like many typical kids. Because walking was so tiring and exhausting, I saved my energy by spending recesses near the school's yellow brick wall. Many of my friends played with me at the wall, and then sometimes they would run off to play on the playground equipment, but I was never upset at them for playing on the equipment. Mostly because I knew it was just what kids do…they play all over the playground. At a very young age I understood that just because certain things were difficult for me, it didn't mean my friends needed to change their routine. Once in a while I walked down to the playground to swing and slide down the slide, but because I was such a slow paced walker I did not get a lot of time on the equipment after reaching the playground. Usually, by the time I reached the playground, the bell would ring sending all the students back to line up, and I had to turn right around and make it all the way back to the school building to line up.

During the wonderful South Dakota winters I would stay especially close to the yellow wall for warmth from the wind. Winter attire was another challenging dilemma for me when it came to returning from recess. I was never as quick at peeling off my wet and snowy layers as my classmates were. I recall an embarrassing moment in first grade when I was dealing with my winter wear. As usual, there were eighteen pairs of rosy cheeks, eighteen pairs of wet mittens, and eighteen pairs of boots covered with snow that surrounded me in our classroom. As a result, I always traveled to a less chaotic area to shed my layers. This safe haven was normally near our big, bright green toy box where all of our playground toys such as jump ropes, basketballs, and footballs were stored. It was difficult for me to sit on the floor and take off all of my winter layers, so I typically sat on the green toy box each day following recess. This particular day I stood up so Nathan, a fellow classmate, could put a basketball away. I thought he had put the lid down but he had forgotten. When he walked away I sat down and fell right into the big green toy box. My feet were pointed straight toward the ceiling, and my hands were tangled up in the vibrant red, green and blue colored jump ropes. I could barely see out of the box as I struggled to get out. I was extremely embarrassed at what had just happened. As I sat in the box I could feel my face starting to get hot, and I knew I was more than likely turning as red as a tomato.

One of my friends saw me with my legs wiggling out from the top of the toy box. Julie was laughing the hardest I had ever seen her laugh as she made her way toward me. She untangled my hands and helped me out of the toy box. I looked around and, just like I thought, seventeen pairs of eyes were looking straight at me. I thought they were thinking I was clumsy and dumb. I also thought they were all going to laugh and make fun of me, but they never did. I guess like everything else with children that age, our attention spans were short and we moved right back into school mode. I do have to say that, thanks to the experience I had on that day, I have always watched my back whenever and wherever I have decided to sit.

Because of the way I was raised, I realized as a young child that just because I had difficulty doing certain things I should never expect my friends or classmates to cater to me during recess or play. As far as I was concerned, we were all allowed to play wherever and with whomever we wanted to during recess. I do have to be truthful though; at times it was difficult seeing all my friends playing on the playground equipment without me, but I knew my body limited me in certain physical abilities. I knew they were still my friends even though I was not playing with them on the swings or slide. I also knew that the sooner I came to terms with what I was going to be able to do physically, the better my life would be.

As children grow up, friendships become stronger and playing at friends' houses and having sleepovers starts to become a part of life. Shortly after second grade, I began to want to spend more time with my friends on the weekends rather than just at school. Being the great mother that she was, my mother was always quick to offer to have my friends at our house. I was content to have friends at my house and never knew that my mother's quick offer stemmed from her not being ready for me to start going by myself to my friends' homes. When children grow, so must parents in their trust abilities. My mother's worries were like any mother's in that she did not want my feelings to get hurt by friends or other children. But like everything else in life, there is a time when letting go is bound to happen. I started going to other friends' houses shortly after fourth grade and began to grow in my independence. While at my friends' houses, the only problem that I ever encountered was staying awake after everyone else had fallen asleep.

In elementary school, the time I spent with friends was filled with building blanket forts, watching tons of Disney movies, playing board games, and eating lots of snacks at my house. We loved to play *Chutes and Ladders*, *Memory*, and *Sorry*. But as we matured into young middle schoolers we loved playing games that definitely fell into the category of "girly games" such as *Dream Phone* and *Mall Madness*. As for games in high school we played more strategic games like *UNO* and *Skip-Bo*. And of course there was a huge amount of laughter and giggling no matter what age we were. Many of my friends would comment on how they enjoyed coming over to my house, because there was usually a lot of eating and talking that went on around my kitchen table. As high schoolers we tried to solve world problems as we ate chips, brownies, M & M's, and drank Coca-Cola, which always magically appeared in front of us to devour. They liked to give my mother a hard time asking if her plan was to get them fat. She responded back to them that they were in high school and were still young and could work it off. There was never a time that my friends went hungry. The rule in my house with friends was that anything not nailed down was up for grabs. My house became my friends' house. Still to this day when my friends come to my house, the same rule applies. They have always been allowed to make themselves at home as much as they wanted to. In high school I could only imagine what our neighbors thought of all the coming and going from our house. It had to be humorous to watch.

I participated in many typical middle school and high school activities with my friends (well, to a point). I never played sports like many of my friends, but I did what I could by cheering them on from the bleachers. As I sat and watched my friends at one middle school volleyball game I was even smacked in the face by a misguided volleyball. My glasses were bent a little but I survived in one piece. I have always supported all of my friends in whatever they do…even if it means being hit in the face with a volleyball. I never have been and never will be a fair-weather friend.

During middle school I went to all of the school dances. Being as short as I am, I would typically get a bird's eye view by sitting on a lunch cafeteria table at these dances to watch all of my friends making fools of themselves out on the dance floor. At one point during a dance I was asked by a classmate if I would dance with him; of course, I said no. I had thought one of my friends had put him up to asking me and I didn't want him to feel like he had to. Also, at that time I was too shy around boys so I made the excuse of not wanting to look like a fool. Later, I was told by my friends that the classmate truly did want to dance with me. The lesson I learned there is that sometimes it's just better to go with the flow when it comes to situations like that.

A Special Angel

I'm thankful that my friends and I have always supported each other during all of our ups and downs in life. One especially challenging situation we all found ourselves in was trying to deal with the loss of our friend Julie Reetz. We were only in sixth grade when we lost Julie to leukemia. We were very young to face something as serious as death. It was inconceivable to us that she was gone. She was a wonderful friend and an extremely brilliant person. Julie cared enormously about people, teddy bears, angels, and God. She showed her belief in angels by drawing, writing, and speaking about them often. She was an incredibly spiritual person and anyone could see that God was a huge part of her life. I admired her for that unquestioning faith at such a young age. I know that was how she handled all of the uncertainty within her life while going through so many tests and chemo treatments for her condition. Julie had leukemia, and she fought as hard as she could all the way to the end. She was in and out of the hospital numerous times for over eight months, so she kept herself extremely busy making angel pins and selling them each day.

Julie was quite the little entrepreneur while in the hospital. She sold angel pins to other patients, nurses, doctors, friends back home, and family members. After she lost all of her beautiful, light brown hair, she started charging her doctor a dollar every time he rubbed her bald head. Julie was a character and had a witty sense of humor. She is a friend I will always cherish and miss for as long as I live. My friends and I were the lucky ones who were able to say she was our good friend.

One of my most memorable memories with Julie was praying with her while on our elementary school playground. She was helping me pray for the strength and energy to be able to attend our weekly mass, despite having just returned to school following Ventriculoperitoneal (or VP) Shunt surgery a week and a half earlier (a VP Shunt is a device which drains the extra fluid in the brain into the peritoneal cavity where the fluid can be absorbed. It's a less-than-pleasant process.) I was working my way back into full days of class when I found out that it was my turn to bring up the offertory gifts during mass that week. When I shared with her that I was afraid I would not be able to physically do it she quickly commented, "Kendra let's pray to God about it. He will help you!" As we held hands and prayed, she helped me feel confident that I was going to be able to successfully carry the offertory gifts for mass. Friday morning of mass came around, and there I was, standing the strongest I had been since surgery, waiting to walk the gifts to the altar, just like Julie and I had prayed for. Her faith has always been an inspiration to me and has helped me when I feel the worries of life consuming me. Whenever that happens, I think to myself, "pray to God, that is what Julie would tell me to do."

There are times I still cannot believe she is not here with us anymore. When my classmates and I graduated from Vermillion High School, as a class we decided to set a teddy bear on a chair on the stage to represent Julie's everlasting presence amongst our class. I still struggle with feelings of missing my opportunity to be with her during one of her last trips home. She returned home from the hospital many times, and she often inquired about how I was doing through our mutual friends. I knew she wanted to see me so we could talk like old times. I always told myself, she is going to be one of those kids that goes into remission, and then everything was going to be okay. I would say to myself, "I will visit her the next time she comes home for sure." Unfortunately, I was too naïve.

I didn't know her last trip home was going to be her final one. Only God knew that. He had provided the opportunity for me to see her one last time. I missed the message He had sent to me, and now I live with that pain every day. At a young age I learned that you never know what tomorrow will bring. We always need to take the time to be with those we love, because when tomorrow comes they may be gone. Missing out on that opportunity with Julie was a difficult way of learning that important life lesson. I wish I had taken the time to tell her how much she meant to me.

I believe that God made Julie an angel. Many times I have felt her presence as my Guardian Angel watching over me, especially when I have needed someone for protection and care. Also, I know that she watches over our friends. I believe she is present all the time just watching our day-to-day lives, helping to guide us through life. Whenever I think of her, I smile and know that where she is now is the best place for her to be. She is walking hand in hand with God, waiting until we meet again.

High School Days

I have so many wonderful memories of my high school career with my friends. One of my first entertaining memories I have as a freshman was the result of a rash outbreak in our school. The whole school got dismissed because there was a mysterious rash causing students to be sick. This early dismissal gave me and two of my friends, Colette and Sarah, time to kill, so we went to my house. I had just gotten my power wheelchair that week so we decided to go for a walk. I came up with a humorous idea of attaching my little red wagon to my wheelchair with a jump rope, so they could sit in it, and I could pull them around the block. I can only imagine what it looked like to people passing by on the street. Two average size freshman girls with their legs folded together to fit in a little wagon as a miniature girl pulled them in her powered wheelchair. As we rounded the corner to head back to my house we saw a man running toward us and to our surprise it was our high school principal out for a run. As he ran by us he smiled and said, "Hi girls." We exploded with laughter after he had passed us, and we all commented, "Well that was awkward!" I still chuckle when remembering that incident.

Another memorable event was at the end of our sophomore year of high school. I had been living in Oakland, California taking part in the clinical research trial when Sarah and Theresa came out to visit me and see what I had been doing for the last three months. We enjoyed sightseeing at Pier 39, Alcatraz, Muir Woods, and Lombard Street in San Francisco. I took them to Children's Hospital & Research Center Oakland, where I was receiving my weekly infusions. They even took part in a movie I was making while I was living in California. I still cannot believe that I got to share part of my experience in Oakland with both of them, especially since we were all just high schoolers. Besides showing what great friends I had, it also showed how amazing their parents were for letting them come to visit me in California. I appreciate their parents very much for allowing them to come.

While I faced plenty of challenges throughout high school, it didn't stop me from enjoying the events that every high schooler has an opportunity to enjoy. For example, I had an amazing time during both my junior and senior proms. I have always loved dressing up in long evening attire, and prom was something I had been thinking about since my middle school days. My Grandma Drew sewed each dress I wore for prom. Junior prom I wore a navy blue off one shoulder dress. I attended prom with my good friend Nicki, and she was a great date. She even loaded my wheelchair into my car in her prom dress and heels...what a strong and skilled young woman. I was even pulled out onto the dance floor by my friend Xavie. She made sure I did not get stepped on while we were out there. We had a blast with all of our friends as we danced the night away.

The following year, for my senior prom, I wore a salmon-colored dress. Because it was my senior prom, I tried to work up the nerve to ask an underclassman to go with me, but I ultimately backed out of it. I was too nervous and a little too chicken to ask him. My friends tried to help me with my nerves, but I just did not have the confidence in myself. They asked me each day if I had asked the guy yet, and I would smirk and shake my head no. I did not have the ability to push myself out of my shell around guys, especially in high school. Also, like in my middle school days, I didn't want him to feel like he *had* to say "yes"; I really didn't want to be a pity date and find out he only went with me to avoid hurting my feelings. A few years later, I found out that he really would have enjoyed going with me, which taught me that sometimes it's best to just take a chance with new experiences, even if the outcome could be scary. There will always be situations in life that fill us with fear or nervousness, but overcoming that fear can lead to some wonderful experiences if we just have the strength to push our boundaries a little bit.

Since I was too nervous to ask my underclass friend, I decided I would see if my cousin Patrick would attend the prom with me instead. As cousins, Patrick and I have always been extremely close, like a sister and brother would be. I knew he would be amusing to go with, and that he knew some of my friends, so he would not feel left out. It was asking a lot of him since he lived in Iowa, and it would be a long trip for him. Being the amazing cousin that he is, he said he would love to go with me. I am blessed to have Patrick as one of my cousins. We both laughed and joked the whole time as the night went on. I especially laughed when my friend Taiana pulled him out on to the dance floor. Patrick has never been much of a dancer, but she got him to attempt one slow dance.

Types of Friendships

I do want to be honest though. I have had my ups and downs with friends, but that is part of being in a healthy and strong relationship with anyone. Many of my friendships have been long-lasting. There has only been one time that a friendship of mine dissolved. It occurred during college. It turned out this friend thought it was a lot of work to be my friend. In all actuality, I believe she did not truly understand me as much as I had given her credit. All through my life I have always worried about my friends feeling like I am a hassle and burden, because I never learned to drive and because it can be challenging for me to walk long distances without my wheelchair. I always try to be very careful—no matter what the circumstances are—to not take advantage of my friends. I never want my friends to think our friendship is ever one-sided. Ironically, what I have always been concerned with was exactly what bothered this specific friend. She felt as though our friendship was one-sided. She felt she was giving more to the relationship than I was, because of all the extra help she had to give me. I have chalked this situation up to being a great learning experience for me. This was the first time I had ever had a friend basically say to my face that being my friend was not worth the hassle. Life is all about gaining wisdom and moving forward for the betterment of life. I know how lucky I am to have the amazing friends that I have now and I will never take them for granted.

Besides this one individual, I have met some incredible people while attending college. These friends have pleasantly surprised me with the close connections we share. Many of these new friends and I have been able to click as though we have known each other forever. Each friend has a special uniqueness that adds to my life and to our friendship together. I believe that being able to confide in each other is what a true friendship is all about, and I can say that I am able to do that with all my friends, no matter when our friendship began. I have many similarities with many of my friends despite my different height and mobility issues. It is amazing, but those things do not seem to hinder my relationship with my friends. Like high school, these new friends come pick me up and we go do things on our own like any other typical twenty-somethings do. I am tremendously fortunate to have friends that look past my small stature and my wheelchair to see only me, and for that I am thankful. There are not a lot of people—no matter who they are and no matter what they have had to deal with in their lives—who are able to say that they have such awesome friends.

The friendships I have are as important to me as my family relationships. I treat my friends as though they are my family members. I think the reason I do this is because I never had siblings, which is why I cherish my connection with each of my friends so much. I would do anything and everything in my power for my friends.

Belief of a Friend

Words of thoughtfulness and understanding
　　come from you,
Creating a feeling in me that it's not impossible
　　to discover love.

Allowing myself to dream and hope that my time of
　　companionship is soon due,
Opens my heart to new possibilities, because I know
　　God guides from above.

The confidence that I've gained in myself from our
　　friendship is a clue,
That I must release my true self as if I have the freedom
　　of a flying dove.

Recognizing all the many qualities I have to offer in a
　　relationship you've helped me to see,
All I have to say to you is that I am blessed to have a
　　friend like you – who believes in me.

Written in March 2009

Chapter 6

*"Adversity causes some men to break,
others to break records."
-William A. Ward*

Educators with Impact

Forming My Future

Throughout life, each of us has had excellent individuals that have made a huge impact in our lives. These are people we never forget about as the years pass by. And hopefully we take time to tell these people how much of an impact they've made on our lives. If you've never done this, I sincerely hope you'll do it in the future. Personally, I have made it a practice to let others know just how much I have gained from their presence in my life. I've had numerous people help me become the successful person I am today and I truly want them to know that.

My love for creative writing began as a fifth grader with my teacher, Mrs. Haggerty. She created a writing environment that was fun for all of her students and provided the opportunity for us to learn from each other. We had weekly workshop time where we shared our current writings with our small group. Mrs. Haggerty helped us when we could not come up with new ideas. If we were stuck with wording, she was always there. I always looked forward to writing workshop so I could become a more skilled writer. Because of Mrs. Haggerty, I began to imagine that someday I would write a book. She helped me feel as though the notion of writing a book really wasn't impossible. Mrs. Haggerty became our sixth grade language arts teacher the next year. During that year, which was spent learning even more from Mrs. Haggerty, I was fortunate enough to have a poem published in Prairie Winds, which is a South Dakota publication project that works to promote student and teacher writings. I credit Mrs. Haggerty for inspiring that creative spark within me and helping me strengthen that creativity.

Math: My Sworn Enemy

I am a person who knows where my weaknesses lie in many aspects of life. People always come upon certain subject areas where they either excel or struggle. All throughout school, no matter which grade level I have been in, math has not been my friend. I have always had to work extremely hard in understanding the concepts. Fortunately, there were two amazing math teachers in my life who both aided me in successfully completing their classes. Mr. Moore and Mr. Anthofer made math understandable and relatable to all their students – especially me. These two teachers had a great deal of patience with all of their students. As a student, I was never afraid to ask questions in their classes or to stop by after school to receive help on homework. I was fortunate to have Mr. Moore as my seventh grade teacher and Mr. Anthofer as one of my high school math teachers. These teachers recognized that I was not someone who picked up math quickly, but they knew I still could do well with guidance and a clear understanding.

Both teachers were comical during class, which always kept it lively. I remember Halloween in seventh grade when Mr. Moore dressed up as a hippie for the Halloween holiday. Even before school had started he got into the Halloween spirit by walking the halls with his big boom box by his ear with 70's music blaring. Later that day when it came to my math period, he played a few 70's songs quietly in the background as we worked on our homework. He stayed in character the entire day.

In high school we were only required to take three math classes, but I decided to take four when I found out Mr. Anthofer taught Pre-Calculus. I had already taken Algebra I from him as a freshman and his ability to help me understand algebra made me confident that I could succeed in Pre-Calculus with his help. (I would have never even given Pre-Calculus a second thought if someone else had taught it.) Mr. Anthofer had a great sense of humor with math, and he was always very truthful about the subject. I remember asking him when I was going to use a certain formula/equation in my future, and he laughed and smiled with an honest answer. "Never Kendra, I am just teaching this because it is part of the curriculum and it says I have to." I remember finding that amusing because I was thinking he was going to give me some lame teacher excuse instead of his comment. To this day I appreciate his honest response, because it was a sign of respect toward my classmates and myself.

After enrolling in Augustana College and getting in the middle of the required math classes (which certainly weren't easy), I asked myself, "Where are Mr. Moore and Mr. Anthofer when you need them?" I needed them badly during those difficult college classes. I got through each class, but it was a challenging battle for me. In every math class I took, I barely ended up with a C. Those classes gave me even more admiration for both my middle and high school math teachers because of how well they motivated their students with such an unexciting subject. While math is a tough subject for many students, Mr. Moore and Mr. Anthofer had a knack for getting the message across to all of their students. I am not sure if they are aware of the impact they had on my math career beginning in middle school and through high school.

Mr. Anthofer had a profound impact on my life beyond math as a freshman. At that time I was dealing with health issues, and he could see that I had daily challenges even with the easiest tasks, such as turning pages of my book and writing down my answers. What I most recall is when he talked to me after class and said that when I had to take a test I would sit at his desk from that point on. At that time I was not aware of it, but my energy was decreasing, and he saw me slowly declining while taking my tests. He told me to tell him what I wanted written down as I went through each problem on the test and he would write it. As I look back now I can see how much ground I was losing, but he never made me feel like I was in trouble because I needed to change the way of getting my work done. I admire him because some teachers might have seen that problem in me and sent me to the resource room for them to assist me instead of taking on the challenge of working with me himself. I am so grateful to him for taking it upon himself to work with me.

I want to thank both teachers for treating me with the respect they gave all their students. I also want to comment that I never felt like they thought I was unable to reach my goals, even though I wasn't the best math student. I do have to say my overall experiences at Vermillion Middle School and Vermillion High School were pretty awesome. I was looked at for who I really was and not as a small, wheelchair-bound person. I am a very lucky girl, and I recognize it. I was never made fun of, and I believe one reason for that was because students saw the teachers' belief in my ability. These two teachers contributed to my positive experience, because of how they took a challenging subject and assisted me in my learning experience.

In addition to Mr. Anthofer, my high school years were filled with others that were incredible teachers. I had the privilege of learning from Mr. Gault in two different classes, English 1 and Composition. I thoroughly enjoyed his classes because of how he interacted with us as students. He was another amazing teacher who treated us with respect and was truly interested in what we had to say. Mr. Gault never made me feel like I was any different from my classmates.

My Continued Love for Writing

One of my freshman classes was Mr. Gault's English 1 class he taught his first year out of college. As freshmen, we were required to take English 1 and had to write a research paper called the I-Search Paper. We all dreaded the I-Search Paper, because we had heard horror stories of how much researching it took to meet the requirements of the paper. Mr. Gault had stressed with us that we were going to be working on the I-search for most of the year so we should pick a topic we were extremely interested in. I went back and forth with ideas, until one day he asked how much I knew about my medical condition. I explained I knew some, but not tons, and would be interested in learning more about what effects my condition were really having on me. That was the beginning of me fully comprehending Mucopolysaccharidosis Type VI. I was surprised at all the information I discovered about MPS VI. It was tough at times seeing that my characteristics were tied to the condition rather than being just my own challenges. For the longest time, I thought my large nose, thick lips and my small, widely spaced teeth were just *my* personal characteristics. Of course, there were many symptoms I did *not* have which made me realize that many of my unique characteristics were simply mine. I gained a lot from the experience of writing that paper. I thank Mr. Gault for giving me the idea to research Mucopolysaccharidosis Type VI because I grew during the process, both with my writing and in my personal understanding of what makes my body tick.

In Mr. Gault's composition class that I took as a junior a couple of years later, taught me how to be wordy with my detailed descriptions in my writing. I have constantly been told through my six years of college that I am wordy. I guess Mr. Gault opened up a side of me that does not know where to stop. I laugh when people tell me that I am wordy – that's just me I guess. I learned in his class we all have our own different styles of writing and that we should be confident in ourselves as we write. I look forward to giving him a copy of this book to show him the impact he has made in my life. I still correspond with Mr. Gault periodically through e-mail. I know that whatever I do with my life, he will be a person I will never lose track of.

Two-Way Impact

Interestingly enough, the subjects that some of my favorite high school teachers taught were the subjects that I was least fond of. Mathematics was one and the other was history. World History and U. S. History were the two classes that Mr. Delvaux taught. As a class, in World History, we were allowed to be creative with our projects. A class requirement was to do reports on certain areas and many of us made movies, most of which were interesting, entertaining and, most importantly, creative. History class was continuously interactive every day. Mr. Delvaux was a jokester too. I looked forward to going to a class where students felt free to be themselves, and he promoted that in his classroom.

Mr. Delvaux and I were also able to relate to each other in a different way other than teacher and student. He has a son who was diagnosed with MPS too. Even though his son's condition is not the exact same type as mine, Mr. Delvaux and I were able to talk through our worries with each other. His son was quite young at the time of his diagnosis. I could see it was a hard hit for him to accept as a father, so I did my best to give him hope for his son's future. He was always there when I needed someone to talk to outside of my family. Mr. Delvaux was the only teacher who ever truly knew what I was going through with MPS. I greatly appreciated being able to stop by after school to talk to him. I also loved hearing about what his son was up to.

Every now and again I still get to see Mr. Delvaux and his son while at Sanford Children's Specialty Clinic, where his son and I each receive our enzyme replacement drugs for our different types of Mucopolysaccharidosis. It is always refreshing to see him and catch up on what's going on in Vermillion High School with teachers and students. I also greatly enjoy talking to his son, even though he is very shy with me. I chuckle and smile when Mr. Delvaux tries to get his son to talk to me. I just say if he wants to talk to me he will. And it probably does not help that I am a girl. But I always say "Hi" and reach out to him in case he does want to talk. In his own time I think he will warm up to me.

The Guidance I Needed

There was one more individual during my high school career that helped me tremendously. He probably has no idea how much I continue to appreciate him to this day. Mr. Griffith was one of our high school counselors. He opened my eyes to funding programs that assist students with a disability while attending college. My parents were unaware of the programs within the state of South Dakota. I remember when he brought up to me about applying to Augustana College. I had heard from prior high school teachers who had graduated from there that they worked closely with their students and had high academic standards. I had always known Augustana College had a great reputation as far as colleges go, but was not sure if I was academically prepared for it. Mr.

Griffith is the one who pushed me to apply and told me that I was definitely prepared for Augustana College. The question was if Augustana College was prepared for me.

Mr. Griffith was one of the first adults (besides my parents) in my life that told me that I have a lot to share with the world. I recall him saying to me as I sat in his office unsure of myself, "Kendra you have the potential to impact others in great ways." I appreciated his comment, but at that time in my life I really did not see how my life experiences would be able to help others. Later down the road I discovered just what Mr. Griffith had been talking about. In college, I befriended a guy I would have never imagined I'd befriend. He was unlike me in many aspects, as he was a six-foot tall college basketball player. I quickly learned through our friendship that, despite our visible differences, he too could relate to similar situations I had found myself in. Looking back, I realize now that Mr. Griffith saw the potential for my future of impacting others and sharing my story way before I had ever imagined it. I knew I was going to college to get a degree, but as a senior in high school I had no clue that, by simply being me, I could actually make a difference. I was a typical senior in high school trying to live life to the best of my ability and I was looking forward to seeing where the path of life would take me.

The Never-Ending Impact of Educators

I have been blessed with numerous people in my life, but, as an Augustana College student, I cannot express how incredibly blessed I was to receive an understanding Academic Advisor in my second year of college. My first advisor ended up transferring to another college, so I was forced to develop a new relationship with someone else. I was extremely nervous when I met with my new advisor, because my first advisor understood what it was like to have a health condition. Her son had a health condition, so she empathized with the challenges I had faced. My new advisor ended up being the best support I could have received as a college student.

Dr. Schrader, my second advisor, was my Sociology Academic Advisor and soon began seeing me for who I really was – a person with a great passion for helping others. There were numerous visits with Dr. Schrader that were honest and heartfelt throughout my five years with her as my advisor at Augustana. We visited about classes, life occurrences, dreams, and goals. She became a mentor as I dealt with new experiences in college. Dr. Schrader was another person, outside of my family, who pushed me to expand my comfort zone as a college student. Without her help, I know I wouldn't have had the opportunity to work in many of the great internships I pursued. She had connections with several healthcare field workers, and all of them knew Dr.

Schrader would not have given them my name if she did not think I was a capable individual. She was always truthful and straightforward with me. Dr. Schrader also never downplayed my concerns about my future.

Many times when we conversed she would say that I needed to write a book about all my life experiences and how I dealt with them positively. She would follow up by telling me that I have a profound story of acceptance that is admirable. I typically grinned and remarked that I was not sure if others should admire me, but I valued her kind words. I often explained that someday I had planned on writing a book. She could count on it. Dr. Schrader watched me grow within my independence and achievements as each year passed during college. She commented that from the first day she met me to my last year of college I was a completely transformed person. I was more confident with myself as to who I was, where I was going, how I was going to get there, and how nothing was going to get in my way. Without Dr. Schrader at Augustana I know my college experience would have been entirely different.

Life is full of people who have an impact on us. Some people impact us more than others, but there is no one person who we have encountered who has not left an imprint on us in some way or another. Some of the most important people we meet in life are those who serve as teachers, advisers and mentors. These are just a few individuals from an incredibly long list who have played that role in my life. All of these remarkable individuals always saw me for me. I never felt as though they took pity on me. They had expectations of me throughout school just like all of my peers. I know that is why I have succeeded thus far. I have cherished all the teachers and mentors who God has brought into my life. As I look toward my future I cannot wait to see who else God will bring into it.

Chapter 7

"Be strong and courageous.
Do not be terrified; do not be discouraged,
for the LORD your God will be with you
wherever you go."
-Joshua 1:9

Coming to Depend on Faith

God and Me

Besides my relationships with my family and friends, another key relationship that has had and continues to have a large impact on my life is my faith in God. To say the least, God is a big part of my life. I have had many incidents where I have had to come to depend on God to help me through life-threatening surgeries and other life-changing decisions. And, time and time again, He has always been there. However, I also have had many questions about Him. I believe that a person can trust in God and still have questions about Him. I do not think it makes a person less of a Christian if they have questions. I think having questions about God is part of growing up and maturing in one's faith in

God. The questions I have offer me a chance to learn more about Him each and every day.

As a result of attending St. Agnes Catholic Elementary School, I think my strong belief in God was solidified. When I was in fifth grade it became difficult for me to walk. My classmates and other students in the school thought nothing of it. They just said, "That is Kendra, and she has a difficult time doing all the things that we can do." I was accepted because it was clear that God makes everyone different. I learned that most people will accept me for who I am, but I also experienced, in some instances, that acceptance might not happen immediately. The important thing is that I know I am exactly the way God wants me to be.

Some members of society and, even the medical community, try to impose limits on people with disabilities. They try to say you can't or you shouldn't do something because it may be a little more difficult. We need to decide for ourselves what we feel is important to do in the time we have here on earth. I have stressed throughout the book to not let others tell someone what they can or cannot do. The obstacles people have to deal with throughout their lives come with numerous types of emotions. I believe in these times of emotional trials, we need God in our lives. "For in the day of trouble he will keep me safe in his dwelling; he will hide me in the shelter of his tabernacle and set me high upon a rock" (*Teen Study Bible*, Psalm 27:5). When emotions run high it is often hard to make a clear decision or any decision at all. Looking to God in prayer and also turning to the Bible is often a good guideline. In *The Book of Comfort* by Alvin N. Rogness, he states in a chapter about feeling like you have lost God that, "You had better trust them" (meaning God and the Bible) "instead of your feelings. If you don't you'll be on a rollercoaster, up and down, and you'll have no comfort at all."

Surgeries with God at My Side

I believe that God has always been present in my life. Before many of my surgeries, I tend to get extremely nervous; that is when I ask God to assist me with my overwhelming fear and guide the doctors throughout my surgery. I know that I could not do anything in my life without having trust in God. I know that I would not be where I am today without Him. I have experienced many times in my life where I felt His presence. One specific time when I was fifteen, I had a surgery where the intubation was particularly complicated, and it was remarkable that I even made it through the procedure. I went code blue twice on the operating table, meaning I was not breathing for a matter of minutes. The doctors told my parents that they did not know how I started breathing again, but I know God was with me at that crucial moment. He had decided that it just was not my time to leave my family and join Him. My mother's immediate response to the doctors was, "God has more for her to do here on Earth with us."

Another example of God's presence was when I was chosen to be in the clinical research trial in Oakland, California. I was a participant in phase II of the research trial of my disorder. As part of this clinical research trial, I received an enzyme treatment drug that a pharmaceutical company was trying to get the Food and Drug Administration to approve. The drug was to provide the enzyme my body does not produce. The enzyme's main purpose is to help keep me healthy and strong and to slow down the progression of MPS VI. With such a limited number of potential test participants, I knew God had played a role in my inclusion for the trial. I have faith that events happen for God's reasons only. Sometimes those reasons are easy to understand and sometimes they are more challenging to see clearly.

Often times when we have physical or emotional struggles, spiritual struggles are not far behind. We may find ourselves questioning God, wondering how He could allow terrible things to happen to us, or whether He really exists in a world of such chaos. We wonder why our prayers were not answered and wonder whether or not there is a plan for our lives. I know that I have at times questioned God's plan, especially when my friend Julie Reetz died of leukemia at the age of twelve. As I mentioned before in an earlier chapter, at that young age, death is never on anyone's mind. She was such an intelligent, wonderful, and compassionate individual. It was difficult for me because she was the first person close to me that I had lost. After a while of trying to figure out why she died, I remembered what strong faith she had in God. She also had a strong faith in angels. I believe she is an angel watching over me, our friends, and her family every day and I know that was all part of God's plan for her.

While recovering from surgery when I was sixteen years old, a man from Vermillion suddenly died in the same hospital I was recovering in. It made me question God's plan. I asked my parents why he died instead of me. How did God make the decision to take him away from his family instead of me? I still ponder that question. I have not really come up with a definite answer. The only thing that I tell myself is that things happen for a reason, and I believe in that very much. We as Christians need to remember that Christ suffered in every way, just as we do here on Earth.

It is hard to figure out why certain situations or circumstances have happened in my life, but I believe that all the struggles I have had made me who I am today. I am a true believer that God created me the way He wanted me to be. He has a plan and a purpose for me and I am hopefully living my life in a way that pleases God.

Of course, that doesn't mean there haven't been other times when I've questioned God and His plan for me. The first time I found myself really questioning God was when I coded twice in the previously mentioned surgery. The doctors had to make some *very* important decisions in a short amount of time, and they quickly decided to abort the surgery. Each time after I recovering from coding, the doctors were unsure about how I could've possibly come back to life. After the second revival, the decision was made to take me off of the surgical table. The doctors felt they had lost me twice and did not want to risk losing me for a third (and possibly final) time. They told my parents and me that I would need a tracheotomy before I could ever have any kind of surgery again. (A tracheotomy is a surgical operation that creates an opening into the trachea through a tube inserted to provide a passage for air). It was then that I found myself wondering why God let me get this far. I traveled to a doctor, all the way to Baltimore, MD, only to get my hopes up and not able to have surgery. What would be the reason for us to finally find a doctor who had some answers to my condition—a doctor who confidently told us surgery would be successful—only for the attempted surgery to end in failure?

As it turned out, we later learned from a neurosurgeon that had the decompression followed by the fusion taken place, it would have been more extensive than necessary. The fusion they were planning would have severely limited my ability to move my head and neck to the left or right for the rest of my life. As a result, I never had the fusion. It would have been an unnecessary procedure with lifelong consequences that would have affected my quality of life.

Another time in my life that I asked God what his plan was when I had traveled to Oakland, California, hoping to be accepted into phase I of the enzyme research trial at the Children's Hospital & Research Center Oakland that I mentioned earlier. We had been through most of the tests and were quite sure I was going to be accepted, only to find out after starting my tests that we would have to return home; the research board was concerned that my compression may cause problems for me during the trial. Once again I found myself asking, Why did I get this far, get my hopes up, only to be rejected as a participant in the research trial? Why would we learn about a possible way to improve my condition only to end up being denied participation in the enzyme research trial?

As a result of this letdown, we returned home by way of the University of Minnesota Medical Center, Fairview, to meet with a neurosurgeon. He examined me and said we needed to perform a decompression surgery soon. Within two weeks I had the surgery. It was successful and I immediately regained my strength, and continued to improve over the following year. As I mentioned before, one year and one month to the day following surgery I received a call from Children's Hospital & Research Center Oakland and they told me they wanted me as the first participant in phase II of the enzyme research trial. I returned to California in

March healthy and strong, and this time I knew I would be a participant in the trial. Thankfully, I was accepted! Also, if I would not have gotten to try to get into phase I, I would not have had the privilege of meeting so many kids with MPS VI from all over the United States. All I need to remember is that as long as God is in my heart, my faith and His wisdom will guide my decisions.

Learning from Him

Every obstacle I have come upon has helped me learn more about God, my faith, and myself. I believe the challenges in my life have pushed me to evaluate what I want to do in the upcoming future. If I run into a roadblock, and still plan on achieving my goal, then I need to start looking for a new way of reaching my goal. In my opinion, it does not matter who anyone is or what anyone has been through in life; everyone has had struggles and/or obstacles. Those obstacles strengthen our faith and make us who we are. I believe that God gives us different roads to take; He does not simply tell us what we should or should not do. We have free will, and it is up to us to make the right decisions in life. Philippians 4:13 discusses this message of counting on God for help: "I can do all things through Christ who gives me strength" (Catholic Women's Devotional Bible). As I stated earlier, I can definitely say that I have had my fair share of moments where I question God's plan for me, but again, that is when I realize that I have to trust Him and believe it all will work out in time. I hope I see all the signs He gives me and that I follow those signs as He would want me to. Looking back, I can see where God has put me in the right place at exactly the right time (even if, at that time, I might not have had a clue as to what was going on). I can later see His plan as I look back at events in my life.

Because I trust God has a plan for me, I also feel He has given me gifts to achieve this plan. I consider my God-given gifts to be listening, talking, creativity, my writing ability, and compassion for others. The way I use these gifts is by listening to others as they discuss their life trials and tribulations when they need to talk things out. I enjoy assisting individuals by helping them use their creative side through painting, writing poetry or stories, or making slideshow movies. Sometimes people just need to have someone who makes them smile and laugh periodically throughout a day. I love helping others put a smile on their face. I know how nice it is when others do the same for me. God gives each and every one of us on Earth talents. Some talents are big, and some are small; it does not matter what size our talents are because God loves us all the same. It is our job to do something with those talents. He gives us the opportunity to do great things; we are the ones who have to recognize our talents and use them by putting our best foot forward with our abilities. He is there, but He is going to let us make our own decisions. It is up to us to make the right ones.

Not only does God have a plan for me, but He has a purpose for everyone He creates. He is the Creator; He made everyone the way He desired. He does not create just to create; He has a purpose when doing so.

> "Just as each of us has one body with many members, and these members do not all have the same function, so we, who are many, are one body in Christ, and individually we are members one of another. We have gifts that differ according to the grace given to us: prophecy, proportion to faith; ministry, in ministering; the teacher, in teaching; the exhorter, in exhortation; the giver, in generosity; the leader, in diligence; the compassionate, in cheerfulness" *(The Harper Collins Study Bible,* Romans 12:4-8).

God created us to be interdependent and share our gifts.

I believe that God creates our individual differences for a reason. He does not want three of me or five of someone else. He wants one and only one of me (and only one of you). While reading *The Purpose Driven Life*, I came across a verse that shows His dedication to making us unique: "You saw me before I was born and scheduled each day of my life before I began to breathe. Every day was recorded in your Book" (Living Bible, Psalm 139: 16). This verse demonstrates how much careful and detailed consideration God took while creating each of us. He did not make all of us on a whim. Another verse that deepens my belief that I am just the way God wants me to be comes from Isaiah 44:2a: "I am your Creator, you were in my care even before you were born" (*Contemporary English Bible*).

While in an Augustana College religion class, someone posed the question of whether or not people with disabilities see God in a different light because of their disability. I remember being caught off guard a little, since I was the only one in class sitting in a wheelchair. I wondered if that question was directed toward me or what the person was getting at. Being the shy individual that I typically am in a large group like that, I said nothing. It did not help that I was a freshman not wanting to stick out more then I already did. I know that if the question were to ever be brought up again, I would have something to say. As far as my opinion goes, I do not think a person with a disability should feel differently about God than a person without a disability. Each person has the chance to live a fulfilling life, depending on how they use the gifts God has given them. The verse that I feel supports my conviction is, "There are different kinds of gifts, but the same Spirit. There are different kinds of service, but the same Lord. There are different kinds of working, but the same God works all of them in all men" (*Teen Study Bible*, 1 Corinthians 12: 4-6). I also believe that nothing can separate us from God's love.

It does not matter what we look like or the way we move around Earth. Having a wheelchair or legs that work does not matter to God. He loves us for who we are. "For I am sure that neither death nor life, neither angels nor demons, neither the present nor the future, nor any powers, neither height nor depth, nor anything else in all creation, will be able to separate us from the love of God that is in Christ Jesus our Lord" (*Teen Study Bible,* Romans 8: 38-39).

There is a purpose for everyone on this earth, whether they are intellectually disabled, physically disabled, or "normal." Each person has a gift to give the world; they just need to recognize it and share it with others. Life's lemons can often be bitter, but by using the resources you have – like sugar and water – you can eventually turn the lemons into something sweet, such as lemonade. The same can be said of struggles in life. They might be tough at first, but using your God-given resources and skills, you can make the best of it in a positive way.

HOPE

I have a bad hip.
The doctors say, "She is too small for surgery,
she still has growth in her body."

I don't want to have surgery.
If only there was something else I could do.

I want to run and walk with my friends, like everybody else.
I don't like sitting by myself when my friends are walking and
running around, but I am use to it.

I wish I could walk with them.

I don't like having my parents do everything for me and with me.
I want to be able to do things for myself.

My hope is, someday I will.

Written while in middle school. 1998

Chapter 8

"Life is like a game of cards.
The hand that is dealt you represents determinism;
the way you play it is free will."
-Jawaharal Nehru

Choosing to be Different

It's Just Me Being Me

As a young female with a medical condition who stands only about forty inches tall, I do come across certain challenges at times. These roadblocks, or as I call them, challenges, do not deter me from pursuing my goals and dreams for my life. They may slow me down while I work around them, but they never stop me completely from pressing forward. I have realized throughout my years that no one in our society goes through life without facing obstacles. Some of these obstacles are more obvious, such as a physical disability, and some are private struggles that the outside world never sees. One thing I try to keep in mind is that just because someone may be of average height and might not be in a wheelchair, it doesn't mean their lives are any easier than mine. I often think more people should keep that in mind. Society is filled with people who are not perfect, and our differences are what create our uniqueness. As individuals, we all have different levels of struggles and challenges. Our response to those obstacles is what makes us who we are. That's why I always try to maintain the attitude that when life has the nerve to hand me lemons, I'm making some darn good lemonade with them.

In my case, the physical challenges are easily visible to anyone who looks at me. Being in a wheelchair and being only forty inches tall is pretty much impossible for others to miss. I accepted a long time ago that my size and walking limitations are just a part of what makes me... me. I have been stared at on many occasions and have been asked ridiculous questions by many people, such as how old I am and whether or not I could talk (I can, in case you were wondering), but I don't let it bother me. It is human nature to be curious about others, no matter what age a person is. I have always tried to have a positive outlook on life and a good sense of humor with all that I have to deal with. I know that having the ability to laugh during certain awkward situations makes me feel a whole lot better. My hope is that you too find the humor in those awkward situations when you find yourself in them. I truly believe that if you can laugh at yourself, it makes life less stressful and much easier to handle.

Not-So-Flattering Stares

Some of the typical staring incidents that occur are usually while I am shopping in a mall.   Normally kids walking through the mall are not paying attention to what is coming up ahead of them. As a result of paying so much attention to me (and my wheelchair) and not looking in front of them, I've seen numerous kids smack their bodies straight into a sign or wall. Those are the times when it becomes too difficult not to burst out with laughter. I don't get down on myself when I am stared at because I know society still has a long way to go before children (and many adults) get completely used to people who don't fit the typical notion of what "normal" looks like. There have been countless times where my cousins Amanda and Erinn have been protective of me and get upset when kids are staring at me and have taken it upon themselves to tell the kids, "Please stop staring, it's not polite to do that." I appreciate their concern, but I usually tell them not to worry because it's bound to happen. It especially makes me chuckle when Erinn gets frustrated with the kids because she is nine years younger than me and gets more defensive about people staring at me than even I do. Nevertheless, I love her and Amanda for being that protective and for watching my back for me.

Of course, it is not *always* easy to just ignore the looks and stares. From time to time I do get a little upset when adults are doing the staring, because I feel like they should probably know better. But I know I cannot get disturbed when a child looks at me strangely because perhaps their parents have not taught them the etiquette of social behavior. Seeing people like me—or someone else who does not fit the "normal" description of what a person looks like—gives parents the perfect opportunity to teach their children that no matter what anyone looks like or has been through, everyone deserves the same respect. I am truly passionate about the belief that we should give respect to all, no matter what.

R-E-S-P-E-C-T

I have done a few speaking engagements where I have discussed the topic of "giving respect to all, no matter what." What I try to explain is that giving respect to all, no matter what the situation is or what the person looks like, is necessary to create a better understanding of what makes this world go around. I also convey that *everyone* needs to work toward learning to accept *themselves*, whether they are a person with a disability or not. When you are confident in yourself, the staring will not, and *cannot*, completely destroy you. A friend of mine has told me that he's been stared at because he is extremely tall; meanwhile, I've been stared at because I am exceptionally small. Both of us are secure with ourselves and who we are, so we don't let it bother us. Being different is not an all-bad thing. It makes us unique, and we need to remember that. I like focusing on this thought because many people tend to think that they are the only ones who are being stared at and usually that is rarely the case. I have seen many people being stared at that do not even seem like they would have anything to really stare at. My mother is another person who has told me she has been stared at. She is not sure why, but she still does not let it get to her. It is important for me that everyone understands that people stare at all individuals no matter what the situation is or what one looks like. We are all curious creatures. As my future presses on I would love to share my notion of learning to accept ourselves and ignoring others who stare. One thing I know for sure is that being stared at does not faze me like it did in the past. The key to stares is to be confident in yourself.

Another thing I have noticed over the years is that sometimes people do not think before they speak. People still tend to make judgments before they actually interact with others. A perfect example in society is when people ask an overweight female when she is due to have her baby. This becomes a very embarrassing problem when the female who has been asked the question is not actually pregnant. I still do get a little frustrated about quick judgments, but, unfortunately, it is human nature to make quick judgments most of the time. I just laugh it off and make a joke of it, saying, "If they really knew me they would never make that assumption of me." There have even been times when I don't answer people—people whom I know I will never see again, of course—because I don't want them to feel awkward after I answer them. I laugh because when situations like that happen, I am usually with my mother, and she so badly wants me to inform the individuals of my age and level of education. She says to me, "If people have the guts to ask dumb questions like that, they deserve to feel weird after you answer them." My mother and I have so many funny memories of situations like that, and we sometimes reflect on them when we need a good laugh.

Did You Really Just Ask That?

Throughout my life I have been asked some of the most interesting and ridiculous questions, oftentimes from adults. "Which elementary school do you go to?" "Can you talk?" "Oh, do you work at Achieve (a place in town where many people with disabilities work)? I have received some form of all of these questions and they are all usually stated in a tone of voice that is normally directed towards younger children or people who have challenges understanding and comprehending. When children ask me these questions, I know that it is all part of their growing up experience, and it never bothers me. I normally have no problem with answering anyone's questions because asking questions is the best way for them to learn. Sometimes when adults ask me questions in a certain tone of voice, I am embarrassed to answer them. The reason I get embarrassed is not for me; I am more embarrassed for the individual who has asked the question. They just do not know better. There are many adults who assume things by just looking at me. My embarrassment is knowing that when I actually answer their question they are not really going to know how to react or respond. The expressions on some adults' faces are priceless after I answer their question with, "I am actually an Augustana College graduate," or "I am 27." Their remarks are usually along the lines of, "Oh...Wow...Okay good for you." On many occasions I can see on their face what they are really thinking: *Holy cow, how do I get my foot out of my mouth in this situation?* I never try to make the situation any worse than it already is for them, so I usually smile and let them go in any direction they want. We all have said things or asked questions at times that we wished we hadn't. Sadly, there are some people who just have a tendency to ask more of this type of question than others. When I find myself in a similar situation, I usually learn from my mistakes and try to never let it happen again. Hopefully it has been a lesson learned for them also.

One could say that these questions, whether they are intended to be rude or not, could still be seen as disheartening for someone like me. While I would certainly agree, it still doesn't keep me from living my life the way I want to live it. When I give thought to all of the questions I've been asked (and the reasons they were asked), I quite frequently snicker at the negative questions because they are usually so off-base from what I'm truly capable of accomplishing in life. If I took to heart all these negative questions, I doubt I would have been able to achieve all that I have achieved up to this point in my life. I view these encounters with people as a positive experience because it inspires me to demonstrate to others that not all wheelchair users or small-statured people are intellectually disabled. In addition, I hope I am able to illustrate that people like me are *not* incapable of achieving enormous success such as receiving a high school or college degree, obtaining a fulfilling career, writing a book, and accomplishing dreams. Staying positive in the most difficult times is how I have been able to take on the hand I've been dealt in life without falling into despair.

Never Dwell for too Long

I want to make it clear that, even though I have accepted my limitation, it doesn't mean I never get annoyed. I do have my moments, but I try to not let myself dwell on them for too long. A perfect example of a situation that I had to overcome was when I was in high school. During that time I encountered a counselor who I believe judged me by my appearance. I had stopped in the counselors' office to get help with my class schedule for my junior year. I had always dealt with a certain high school counselor, but that day he was busy with other students, so I went to another counselor for help. I had always thought that this other counselor seemed nice, friendly, and caring. But after our discussion my opinion had significantly changed.

I started talking about what classes I wanted to take for the following school year, and as we talked I began to feel like a four-year-old child because of the way I was being talked to. I had explained that I wanted to take American Heritage and Algebra II my junior year, ignoring the counselor's "speaking to a child" tone of voice. The response I received was that "Students who take those types of classes are thinking about college in their future." She then went on to add that for any student to be accepted into American Heritage, they needed to obtain a signature from a teacher who felt they were capable of taking the class. I smiled and kindly pointed toward the signature I already had from a teacher. I also nicely added that I planned on going to college in my near future. I then wrote all the classes down that I wanted to take and gave them to the counselor to enter into the computer. As soon as that was done, I turned right around toward the door and left the office with a very uneasy feeling in the pit of my stomach.

My nervous feeling was the result of what she had said to me about students who had planned on attending college. Being talked to as if I were a young child made me start to lose my confidence. I did not know how to respond to her statement about college. The statement made me rethink and doubt my decision about going to college. I began to ask myself if I was capable. I did not like the way I was feeling about myself after our discussion. It was an unfamiliar feeling for me, because I had never thought I wouldn't attend college. I always thought it was simply the next step after high school. When I had previously talked about college with my parents, they had never told me it was a ridiculous idea. They always had confidence that I could do well and would excel.

It did not take long for me to decide that college was the right step for me. My parents and I also came to the conclusion that this particular counselor did not really understand my goals, or, more importantly, *me*. I thought about everything that I had done and the awards I had received, like maintaining a 3.6 GPA, becoming a National Honor Society member and winning both a Governor's Leadership Award and a "Yes I Can" Award. I recognized that the awards were not just handed to me. I have worked hard for all the accomplishments I received in my life. To say the least, the statement, "Don't judge a book by its cover," is very applicable to me and my life. That high school counselor's particular perception of me not being college material is just one of the many misperceptions I have encountered, and I know it's a misperception many other people like me experience every day. These judgments were made by my book cover; made by how I looked and not by my ability as a student. Since my experience with that counselor, I have looked back at the situation and can honestly say that I am not angry with her. She helped me to understand how others might see me and that experience reminds me to never let others' beliefs of my perceived "lack of ability" influence me. The experience motivated me to do something great and to try to achieve all of my immediate life goals.

There were also some incidents while attending Augustana College where I experienced unfair judgments made of me. There were a couple of professors that made comments that were extremely upsetting to hear. I was told that I like to take the easy way out and that I might not be cut out for graduate school. There was also an incident where a professor took me aside and questioned if I had actually participated in a group activity as much as I said I had, because my group told him otherwise. He assumed what the other students told him was fact before talking to me. On behalf of the professors, I am not sure they were even fully aware of how those comments truly affected me. At the time, it was a huge blow to my self-esteem and integrity. Those comments have become fuel for me to prove to others that I have as much ability as any other person. My integrity is all I have, and I never want anyone to doubt my character. I want people to realize that a person should not be able to tell someone else what they can and cannot do. While I do believe it is appropriate to inform a person that college, graduate school, or some other type of training might be challenging, they should never try to put limits on a person. Encouragement and support are what people need, not limitations.

These particular situations I found myself in did not necessarily occur because I am a person with a disability. The disheartening fact is that society is filled with people who are not fully aware of how certain comments and situations could affect someone else's life. The large blow to my self-esteem and integrity could have happened to anyone, and I am sure it has happened to plenty of other people plenty of times. Countless people have been hurt by unfair comments, but no matter who you are or what you look like, it is important that you remember to never accept others' limitations. We simply need to remember that *we* are the only ones who make the decision to let others' notions affect us; we can succumb to their comments *or* make the choice to keep pursuing our own life dreams and goals.

As a result of these situations, I have learned that dwelling on the negativity of life's challenges really doesn't get me anywhere. I think everyone is allowed a certain time to be upset with situations, but then they need to turn the negative into positive. Complaining about what difficulties I have to deal with or being frustrated by the things I can't do is neither productive nor healthy. I view my physical limitations as blessings. Paul wrote in Romans,

> "Therefore, since we are justified by faith, we have peace with God through our Lord Jesus Christ. Through him we have obtained access to this grace in which we stand, and

we rejoice in our hope of sharing the glory of God. More than that, we rejoice in our sufferings, knowing that suffering produces endurance, and endurance produces character, and character produces hope, and hope does not disappoint us, because God's love has been poured into our hearts through the Holy Spirit which has been given to us." (Romans 5:1-5, RSV).

Negative Nellies

I have run into many people throughout my life who have been, as I put it, "Negative Nellies." No matter the circumstances, they see the glass as half empty. Interestingly enough, the individuals I have encountered with the "Negative Nelly" outlook have been people both with and *without* disabilities. This just shows that, no matter what a person has to deal with, they can still have an extremely negative outlook on life. The direction in which you want your life to go is determined by your outlook and your attitude. When a person is mad at the world for something that has happened to them or an obstacle that has been put in front of them, their attitude will inhibit them from being able to overcome that obstacle. I would love to be able to share my message of "Your Attitude On Life Determines Your Future" with youth groups, high schoolers, college students, adults, and/or individuals with a disability. I am exceptionally passionate about delivering the message to keep thinking positively about yourself, no matter your life circumstances.

I have conversed with people who see only negative, and I usually explain that if you look at life in a negative way, then, without a doubt, life will be unfulfilling and unsatisfactory. Resulting in a self-fulfilling prophesy. Many people could easily be negative with all that they have to deal with day in and day out, but as I mentioned before, it's how we respond to those challenges that makes the difference. Even though we encounter obstacles, I want people to keep in mind that we should never give up on our dreams and goals. Having ambition is how you make life interesting. Believing in ourselves and remembering that life is what we make it is the key to reaching where we want to be in life. We need to find ways to work around these obstacles in our paths to keep moving forward and achieve our dreams.

All through my life I have wanted to be defined by my personality and what I can do, rather than what I cannot do. I know that if I plan on reaching all my aims, I must use my God-given strengths. Life is tough no matter who anyone is, what anyone looks like, or what anyone wants to pursue in his or her future. My future is bright if I see it that way. I have a dream of someday getting the opportunity to share my life's challenges and experiences with others by traveling around and speaking to others. I would love to speak with individuals who have similar challenges. It would be an amazing feeling to be able to inspire others who have to face challenging obstacles in life. I want them to know, "When life hands you lemons, make lemonade." Or my twist on that phrase, "When life hands you lemons, turn right around and squeeze those lemons to make the _BEST_ lemonade possible." I know that my message of being positive and having a positive attitude during tough times is an important message to many. I have always had high expectations for myself, and I know that is why I have come as far as I have. Sometimes people need to be reminded that life is full of ups and downs for everyone. Just because people can see my wheelchair, it doesn't mean that someone sitting next to me in a regular chair is any less challenged than I am. We all have dreams that we want to achieve, and none of us should let others steer us away from reaching them.

WHY?

There is that short girl again.
She looks like she is two, but
she talks like a teenager.
Why is she so small?
Is she normal?
She must be odd?

Why do people stare at me?
I am as normal as everyone else.
This is the way God wanted me to be.
Why can't people realize that
even though I am small, I am
creative, generous, friendly, and giving.

Written in 1998

Choosing How to Live Life

I believe that life is what one decides to make it;
And one should take each day in stride, as it comes.
When daily troubles arise, don't just give up and quit!
Instead one should march to the beat of one's own drums.

I believe looking at what one has been blessed with is key;
Humor, optimism and faith are the perspectives I choose.
This allows me to persevere and retain a spirit that's carefree!
Without a lighthearted attitude, I'd be the one that would lose.

I believe life is too short to dwell on the negative. We need to trust.
God surrounds us every day with His guidance, compassion, and love.
We need to open our eyes and hearts to let Him in. We must!
When we give ourselves to Him, He smiles from above.

I have placed a lot confidence in God, which has helped me grow.
I have come this far in life because of believing in Him, I know.

Written February 2009

November 3rd, 1984:
Proud father holding me
for the first time.

Learning to walk on the
Drew farm.

Playing in
Grandma Drew's
cupboards.

Teaching my dad
how to cheer!

Christmas morning
with my mom at
the Gottsleben
house.

Celebrating my 3rd
birthday party.

Trying to act like I can read… I have always loved books!

Grandpa Gottsleben, me, and Grandpa Drew

Grandma Drew, me, and Grandma Gottsleben

A Minnie Mouse themed birthday party!

Playing with my favorite doll.

Anxious to open all of my Christmas presents!

Rolling around at a skating rink party with friends.

My 1st grade class.

5th grade Halloween school party.

Waiting for my friends to show up for my birthday party in 6th grade.

Hanging out with my Gottsleben cousins.

Joking around with my youngest Drew cousin.

Spending time with two of my Drew cousins.

Gottsleben Grandparent's 50th Wedding Anniversary!

Two great teachers who were with me when I was presented the "Yes I Can" award.

Laughing with one of my
friends who also has MPS VI

My friends and I at
my Junior Prom in 2003.

Having ice cream in Oakland, CA with
my friends who also have MPS VI.

Trip to San Francisco in front of the Golden Gate Bridge.

Taking in the view of the coast during my stay in San Francisco.

My wonderful cousin and I at my Senior Prom in 2004.

May 2004: Excited to graduate from high school with all of my friends.

Just being silly me!

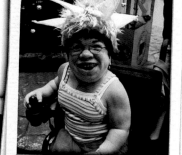

At my "Heaven on Earth," the New York City M&M Store, with my two Drew cousins.

Relaxing on the couch with my younger Gottsleben cousins.

Posing with my dad and his parents, my Gottsleben grandparents.

Drew relatives gathering at my Uncle's Navy band performance.

One of the greatest friends ever!

Drew Grandparent's 60th Wedding Anniversary.

Times Square...a night I will always remember with all the unbelievable colors everywhere!

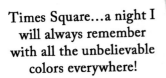

Brooklyn Bridge, NYC!

Quality time with my Grandma Gottsleben and aunt.

With friends at a MPS VI conference in Minneapolis, MN.

My proud father and I on my College Graduation Day.

College graduation party chilling with my awesome friends.

Posing with my proud mother on my College Graduation Day.

The next mini South
Dakota Senator.

At the U.S. Capitol in
Washington, D.C. with
Drew family members.

Speaking at the
TEDx Sioux Falls
event.

Two of my cousins that will always have my back no matter what.

The BEST nurses EVER!!!

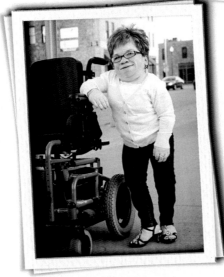

Always going to choose to make lemonade in my life, no matter what.

Chapter 9

*"The more difficulty one has to encounter,
within and without,
the more significant and the higher in inspiration
his life will be."*
-Horace Bushnell

Facing Challenges

Small Hurdles

I have had to deal with inconvenient struggles on a daily basis for much of my life. Most people see these inconveniences as challenges or obstacles, but I don't necessarily see the struggles as challenges because they are sort of just part of my life. Sometimes I don't even realize how inconvenient something is until someone from outside my circle points out how much harder I have to actually work. Then again, there are plenty of things I do face on a day-to-day basis that *are* challenging. Opening doors is one of those silly things that not many people think about, but in my case if there is not a push button for the door, it can be a huge obstacle. Opening the door can be done, but it takes a lot of time, strength in my arms, and good calculations. The calculations come into play as I shimmy back and forth with my wheelchair trying to open the door while at the same time entering the room. (In these cases, I often think about how proud my middle school and high school math teachers must be as I put my geometry skills to good use.) Though not *impossible* for me, the process certainly isn't fun. I have also gotten a lot better at asking for help when I think a door is going to be extremely heavy to open. Countless times people have made comments about how they are amazed at my physical strength and ability to open doors. I grin at them and usually say, "My arms may look skinny and scrawny, but they are more powerful than they look!"

Thankfully, society has realized how troublesome doors can be, because more and more places are installing push button door openers, which are truly helpful for people in wheelchairs, the elderly, and others who might not have a lot of strength in their arms. I do not expect the push buttons everywhere, but they do make life a lot easier. What also helps is when people are kind enough to open doors for me. About seven years ago I began noticing that there are some people with disabilities who get offended when a person tries to help them by offering to hold open a door. Once I even had someone tell me that they do not like it when people offer to help, for example, offering to pick up their pencil that had fallen. The concept of getting upset at these kind gestures is unbelievable to me. I do not see their assistance as a sign of them thinking that I am incapable of opening a door. I see it as someone being kindhearted and considerate. Those individuals who are so quickly offended when anyone helps them out need to take a step back. They need to take the time to see that people help others no matter what circumstances the person being helped may be in. I have seen people assisting others whether the recipient of help is short, tall, in a wheelchair, or walking. It is just the right thing to do as a human being.

Besides dealing with ever-challenging doors and other physical demands, my social life has also been impacted as a product of having MPS VI. It affected me more as I ended my high school years and began college than it did when I was younger. As a result of not having my driver's license, trying to meet up with my friends has been difficult at times. I have been blessed, because most of my friends — both in high school and in college— have no problem coming to pick me up when we want to get together. I am not sure many people can say they are that fortunate. My mother has also been incredible with her willingness to take me places so I can meet up with my friends. During high school my mother would even let my friends take our family car so that I could take my wheelchair wherever we went. She trusted my friends, and my friends never broke that trust. They are pretty special people. I laugh sometimes because when you become friends with me you must be trained in how to load my wheelchair into an SUV or van. Being my friend is not as easy as being a friend of someone who does not have such limitations. That is why I love my friends so much – they've never cared about the baggage that tags along with me. When I tell them thank you for coming to get me they always tend to follow with, "Kendra, isn't that what friends are for?" A statement like that truly only comes from *real* friends.

Challenges come in all different shapes and forms for each and every one of us. Sometimes people are able to recognize what could potentially be a challenge for another individual and sometimes it may never cross their mind. An interesting challenge I face that some people might not have ever considered is when I answer the phone or make an outgoing call. The dilemma I find myself in more times than I would like to count is people hearing my voice on the phone and thinking I'm not who I say I am because of my "child-like" voice. When I answer my cell phone, many people mistake my voice for a little girl answering "my mommy's cell phone." I have also had individuals ask me to give the phone to "my mommy" when in actuality I am the one who called the insurance company or doctor's office. I've come to recognize that assumptions will be made with me on the phone and many times I dread having to make important calls like that as a result. I realize it is just another unique characteristic of mine that

I have to deal with in life. As a result, I typically try to answer my cell phone or make a call with a more professional tone and language. I have begun to get used to it, so I'm usually ready for it by simply trying to answer the phone saying, "This is Kendra Gottsleben, how can I help you?" I have even had someone who called me regarding a medical prescription in which she commented to me, "Wow you are twenty-five…you sound like you are seven." I laughed quietly and remarked, "Yes, I am familiar with that assumption, I have received that reaction several times." I look at situations like this and try to see the humor in it. Many of my Mucopolysaccharidosis Type VI characteristics I do not have control over, but that cannot stop me from moving forward in life, and I make the choice to confidently move forward every day.

The circumstance of not having a driver's license has been a huge challenge for me when it comes to everyday life too. Since my mom still works, I cannot depend on her to give me rides anytime I need her to, so I depend on a local transit system. This is a service for people with disabilities who need transportation around town. I know I am very fortunate that my town has a transit system like this, but as a person who enjoys her independence, sometimes this service can be frustrating. Using this bus system requires calling a day ahead of time for scheduling rides. There is also a 30-minute window where I may be picked up, but there is no guarantee that they will actually show up on

time. I am also not always guaranteed that they will drop me off
right away or on time if there are other passengers on the bus,
which often means I either arrive way too early for things or
worse, way too late; there is rarely a happy medium. So, while it is
great having this service, it does limit my independence and the
ability to be spontaneous. This inability to be spontaneous was
extremely frustrating at times, like when my college professors
would cancel class at the last minute and I would not find out until
I had already gotten to the classroom door. Many times it was my
only class for that day or I would have to wait two to four hours
until my next class. Nobody enjoys having a class or meeting
cancelled at the last minute or being stood up by someone, and for
some people with disabilities, it can be more than a slight
inconvenience. Sometimes when I ride this transit system, I feel
more disabled than I really am. This feeling comes from the fact
that many times I do not see myself as truly a person with a
disability; rather, I see myself as an individual who needs to use a
powered wheelchair in larger spaces to get around and who might
need a little extra assistance in reaching objects. Not being able to
time my life, or go where I want to, exactly when I want to, makes
me feel powerless sometimes. But I do not have a lot of choice in
those incidences, and it has taught me that it doesn't do any good
to dwell on what I cannot control.

My independence and inability to be spontaneous has also affected my life in ways other than transportation. Being dependent on others has directed much of my life in the fact that I have not been able to do all the activities that many of my peers have been able to, such as making a quick trip to the mall on my own, meeting up with friends for dinner and drinks on the spur of the moment, or just popping by a friend's house randomly. Even the simplest occasion of meeting up with friends has at times led to the feeling of disappointment in not being able to act the actual age I am with my peers. Then again, over the years (from high school through college and even now) I have always tried to avoid putting myself in social situations where I might feel uncomfortable with what is occurring. And as a result of my inability to act spontaneously, I have been able to gain other types of satisfactions in life. Not being free to be spontaneous has helped me develop the ability, even at a young age, to always have a Plan A and a Plan B for situations or events in my life. Being a planner has benefited me in that I've become realistic in what I can and cannot obtain. Another advantage is that I have not done anything stupid in high school or college that I have later regretted. That is not something most twenty-somethings can say. Life has times where one has to distinguish that not *everything* is feasible with limitations and that is where my optimistic outlook on life comes into play. For every negative in life there is usually a positive that comes right along with it. You just have to be looking for that positive.

College Life

Another aspect of being independent has to do with living arrangements. All throughout college I lived at home, so I did not really make as many friends at college as most students typically do. There were pluses and minuses with those circumstances, but I was mostly fine with it. On the positive side, I got to see my family members more and did not have as many distractions like friends wanting to hang out in a dorm to take me away from my studies. One downside was that I did not get the same opportunities to meet new friends. Class interactions with peers are not the same as dorm interactions. Living on campus makes people more aware of what events are going on within the college community, which I was never fully aware of. Much of that is my fault, as I could have worked harder at getting more involved. But I think that if it really bothered me to a devastating effect, I would have done something about it. I believe that, because I have continued such extremely close connections with many of my high school friends, I never felt like I was without friends, even though they went to college in different states. I still missed doing things on a normal basis with friends, but I never let myself dwell on it.

The last couple of college years was when I finally started meeting new friends. I think at the beginning of college I was at a different point in my life, and as the years went by I started developing into a new and independent person who was ready for new friends to mix in with my old friends. Now some of my closest friends are the ones I met during college and have maintained a relationship with them ever since.

Men, Self-Confidence and Me

One inevitable challenge of growing up is developing relationships with members of the opposite sex. Not surprisingly, MPS VI doesn't make this challenge any easier to deal with, and it has certainly affected my social interactions with males throughout my life. This has been true since high school and has been more of an issue with my self-confidence than anything else. The issues were more about me not having the confidence to push myself out there to interact with guys. Even though I am typically an open person, I've always seemed to sort of shut down and become quiet around guys my age. However, over the years I have learned to change my immediate reaction to a guy talking to me from negative and nervous to positive and confident. One of the biggest self-confidence issues I have had to overcome is realizing that guys my age are not simply talking to me because they feel sorry for me, but rather because they think I am an interesting and enthusiastic person. This revelation presented itself when I put myself out there through Facebook instant messaging and began striking up conversations with old Vermillion school classmates and fellow

Augustana classmates who were guys. Then, after that first step, I began moving forward with pushing myself out of my comfort zone into face-to-face conversations. As our conversations would take place I could see that they saw me as "Kendra" and not "Kendra, that girl who is in a wheelchair." Sometimes I *really* put myself out there and asked what their impression of me was throughout our years of school together. I was always pleasantly surprised because they typically commented that I seemed confident, upbeat, enthusiastic, and they said I never came across as if I felt sorry for myself. These statements showed me that I was coming across to others the way I had hoped – with an attitude of "Life is what we make it!" Hearing those remarks from guys made me realize that, for the most part, people see me in the way I have always desired. Keeping true to who I really am has been apparent to others more than I had ever realized.

I can thank many of my guy friends who have helped me see that opening up around them is just as easy as interacting with girls (well, sort of). I have been told that it does not matter if I have not dated anyone yet; it simply means the right person has not come along. I chuckle at that comment because I have never quite seen the positive side of never having dated someone. I sometimes think that I may never meet a guy who will want to date me or even marry me. I know that there are guys who like me a lot, but there is a difference between being a friend and being someone who wants to be in a long-term relationship with me that could lead to marriage.

What I try to remember, when these thoughts come to mind, is that there are many people in society that have the same feelings and worries. Nearly everyone, at some point in their life, ponder the questions "Will I get married?" "How old will I be?" "Do I have a soul mate?"... It seems more people are getting married later in their lives, in their thirties or forties even, and I even have some friends who wonder if they will ever marry; however, despite our plan to "take the plunge" or not, these questions always seem to arise. This monumental life decision is a frequent topic of conversation with many of my good friends. During these girl-talks, I confess to them that my confidence level with guys has grown in recent years, but I still have a ways to go.

Like most people my age, I have a dream to have my own family someday. However, when we are pondering these great questions of life, I think it is important to remember God is the only one who knows whether that will or will not happen for me, or anyone for that matter. Maybe there is a husband in my future and I have yet to meet him. All I can do is make the most of God's plans for me, have faith in his vision for my life, and see what happens.

A Million Butterflies

I've mentioned before that I want to travel and share my life experiences and positive outlook on life with others. The amusing issue with this dream is that I still get extremely nervous talking in front of people. This nervousness has been with me ever since I was in elementary school. As students in a Catholic elementary, we had to take turns reading the liturgy and petitions, or taking up the offertory gifts at our weekly mass. I never volunteered for the readings. I always volunteered to take up the offertory gifts. The reason I did not want to speak was because I was so afraid I was going to mess up while standing in front of everyone in church. This feeling stayed with me all through middle school, high school, and college. Speaking has gotten easier for me in some situations when I am talking about topics that are close to my heart. I always type out exactly word for word what I am going to say on paper, and I always have it with me during the presentation. I do this so I do not get side tracked with some other topic. I know that this technique is a little unconventional, because it looks like I have not practiced and that I am just reading from the paper. In reality it is a safety net for me. I know there is a lot of room for improvement for me to become a better speaker in front of an audience, but who in this world can say that they do not have room to grow?

Surprisingly, even though I get immensely nervous when speaking to a large group, I have had many people tell me that when I actually speak, no one can tell that I am nervous. Usually I am nervous right before I actually speak and for a few minutes after I begin. But usually a few minutes into my presentation or discussion I begin feeling a little more at ease. Even as a child I can remember my parents telling me that I did not sound nervous at all in church. Whenever they told me that, it always made me feel better because I knew that, because they love me, they would have told me the truth if I had sounded awful. At the time, I would tell them that if they could have felt what my stomach was doing as I was waiting, they would have understood that my stomach felt like it was filled with a million butterflies. I have been lucky to never sound like what I am actually feeling at the time. It probably would have been a little embarrassing.

Much like public speaking, singing solos brings on the same nervous, million butterfly feelings. I have to admit, though, that singing a solo publicly is a lot more challenging for me than speaking publicly. For as long as I can remember, singing and music has been something I have always been around with the Drew side of my family. My Grandpa Drew sang throughout much of his life at special events and other unique occasions, including a barbershop quartet, St. Patrick's Day Ceili, funerals, and family reunions to name a few. This music ability was passed down to his three daughters and one son (my mother, Aunt Denise, Aunt Mary, and Uncle Dan). My mother and her sisters were asked to sing at weddings, baby showers, and local Northwest Iowa establishments. Besides these events, they also sang at many family reunions. My Aunt Denise and Uncle Dan are the ones who stuck with their love of music as they both studied music during their college career. Aunt Denise became a middle school music teacher and Uncle Dan became a professional musician in the United States Navy. Fortunately, the love of music has traveled down from generation to generation; I have enjoyed singing since I was a child and still love it now.

When I was fifteen years old my Aunt Denise asked me to sing a solo as she accompanied me with her guitar. It was to be for my Drew Grandparents' fiftieth wedding anniversary mass. When she first asked me I immediately said that I didn't think I could do that with so many people in the church looking at me. My aunt told me that my two other cousins, Isaac and Amanda, were going to sing a duet for Grandma and Grandpa and she knew my grandparents would love me singing for them. I really wanted to sing for my grandma and grandpa because I cherished them so much, but I really did not think that I could pull off singing alone. I decided to learn the song and practice, doing my best to ignore the feelings that I could make a massive mistake with everyone listening to me. I thought about all that my grandparents had ever done for me and decided that singing in church was the least I could do for them. Denise and I practiced every chance we got. The wedding anniversary day came and I sat with Isaac, Amanda, and Denise in church focusing on the words I would soon be singing. Meanwhile, my stomach felt like it was doing back flips all over the place as the time got closer for me to sing. What helped was that we sang up in the balcony of the church, so no one was directly looking at us as we sang. After my cousins sang their duet, Amanda came and sat next to me while I sang the song "Thy Word" by Amy Grant. That simple gesture eased my nerves a great deal. I am proud to say I sang it without a hitch. Many people who attended church that day were very surprised that I was the one singing "Thy Word." They had no idea that I could sing like many of my other family members, and they thought it was someone else singing the last song. Numerous people complimented my grandparents on having such talented grandchildren, which made me smile. I told everyone in a joking manner that was probably the only time they would ever hear me singing a solo for the rest of my life. I love to sing, but I prefer singing with groups. On this occasion, however, I enjoyed singing for my grandparents; I would do anything for them. I made the decision to sing despite my nervous feelings, because I wanted to challenge myself. I am still proud of myself for doing it and doing it well. Challenging ourselves regardless of whether the outcome is good or bad helps us learn key aspects about ourselves for the betterment of our future.

A More Severe Challenge

One of the greatest challenges I've had to overcome occurred when I was a sophomore in high school. As I referenced before, at age sixteen, my energy level was slowly declining and my physical ability to do even simple, everyday activities was deteriorating. This was because of a compression at the base of my skull. The regression was so long and progressive that I had not realized just how much I was losing the ability to do physically.

Because of my noticeable decline in energy and ability prior to my sophomore year of high school, I traveled to Towson, Maryland, where I met with a brilliant doctor who we'll refer to as "Dr. K," Chief of Pediatric Orthopedics at St. Joseph Medical Center. He was scheduled to perform the surgery for my compression when I was an eighth grader. As a result of complications with the intubating process for surgery, he made the decision to stop the surgery and reschedule it for another time. He and the other doctors needed to take time and reassess the nooks and crannies of my throat structure. Just before my rescheduled surgery, Dr. K suffered injuries from a serious fall so surgery was postponed indefinitely and we had to keep waiting. After six months of waiting my family and I found out that Dr. K had actually fallen as a result of a brain tumor, and was working his way towards recovery. Shortly after receiving that call we got the heartbreaking news that Dr. K had suddenly gotten worse and tragically died. The news was devastating to us. He was an amazing person and surgeon, and we felt as a family he was our one and only hope. He was one of the first doctors who treated me as an individual, and directed his questions towards me, not just my parents. He had so much compassion in his eyes regarding me as a patient and a person that I had been overcome with trust and confidence in him.

After his death, my family's hopes were dashed, as we realized at that point we had no clue where to turn or what to do to address my compression. It was clear that if I did not receive surgery, my time on Earth was limited. Realizing that we were in need of a new doctor, my mother decided to call the president of the National MPS Society Organization to see if she knew of any excellent doctors. The president and my mother had a long conversation discussing my slow decline, and it was during that conversation that my mother learned of a clinical enzyme research trial on MPS VI at the Children's Hospital & Research Center in Oakland, California. My mother got the name of the research doctor who was in charge and called him immediately. My age and type of MPS were exactly what they were looking for as a participant in the research trial. As I mentioned before, my mother, father, and I were flown to California a few months later in December of 2000. While in California, I went through countless medical tests to make sure I actually had MPS VI. Sadly, Dr. H, told my parents that the medical review board was worried about my compression issue. I was not going to be allowed to enter the study. The doctor told my parents that if we wanted to take care of the compression issue, I might be considered for phase II as a participant, but he had no idea when phase II would begin. As we packed to return home, my mother was skeptical about receiving the call for the second round of participants.

My mother and I flew to the University of Minnesota Medical Center, Fairview to discuss my compression with a neurosurgeon, Dr. L, and within two weeks I had the decompression surgery. It was one of the most challenging surgeries I have ever had because of the doctors having to work so closely to my spinal cord. I was extremely scared knowing how perilous it was, but I had to put my trust in my team of specialized doctors. Like every surgery I have ever had, it lasted much longer than when working on a non-MPS patient, but all in all, the surgery was a success. Unfortunately, the recovery was a long and drawn-out process. Dr. L said that recovery would take at least a year before everything would be somewhat back to normal.

Those five days in the ICU were extremely challenging days for my parents. I was unable to talk because a tube to help me breathe was placed down my nose and throat while I was in the ICU. I remember an amusing time when my mother and I were trying to communicate using paper and a pen. We were both getting frustrated with each other during this particular time. I wrote a response. She questioned me, and then I repeated what I had written previously. She stated that she had gotten the first part, and said in a pretty firm voice, to not keep repeating from the beginning. This comment annoyed me so much that I decided to take the pen I was writing with and flick it across the room. My mother burst out laughing and commented to a nearby nurse, "Okay, now I know for sure she is getting better because she is getting her attitude back!"

The inability to talk because of tubes was something my parents and I had not thought about when preparing for surgery. My father at times had to leave when the nurses came in to suck the mucus from my lungs. It was hard to watch this specific treatment because I was receiving air to my body manually for a number of minutes. I cannot imagine how difficult it was for them to watch their one and only daughter hooked up to those tubes and machines that surrounded her. Fortunately, I came out of this experience much improved. And after a year of recovery, we actually received the call from Oakland wanting me to return as a participant in phase II of the clinical enzyme research trial; this time I was accepted into phase II. Little did I know how my life would change for the better by participating in phase II of the clinical research trial.

Breaking Through

Another one of the greatest challenges I've ever faced in life also took place when I was a little older – this time as a freshman at Augustana College. The incident itself shook me and my mother so badly that to this day we are still extremely cautious when we go to bed, and getting over the effects of it have been an obstacle I never would have imagined I'd have to overcome.

When we first moved to Sioux Falls, our house in Vermillion had not yet sold, so my mother and I decided to rent a house from Augustana College. This house was directly across the street from campus. Early one day at about four in the morning, my mother and I heard three loud pounding noises on our front door. Interestingly enough, I am usually a sound sleeper, so for me to hear the noise must have been a sign that God was with us. I called out to my mother asking her if she had heard what I heard and she quickly said yes and to be quiet. The pounding started up again, and this time there was a man's voice yelling that we needed to let him in. At this point my mother was out of bed talking through our living room door, telling them they had the wrong house. This man was persistent and kept yelling, "Let us in! We're from the Sheriff's department!" This went on for another couple of minutes with my mother yelling, "You are not from the

Sheriff's department, look at the house number; you have the wrong house!" After yelling at this individual my mother ran into my room asking me for my cell phone because it sounded like he was starting to kick the door. She was right. After throwing her my cell phone, she went back out to the living room and found not just one man but four men dressed in camouflage from head to toe and wearing ski masks. One of the men even had a rifle pointed directly toward my mother as she entered the living room. Besides the man holding the gun, one man was walking through our kitchen and back to the living room laughing and smiling as he repeated the Sheriff story. The other two men were just standing and watching as if they were the backup in case we got out of hand. I was so amazed at how calm my mother was as she stood up against the wall with the gun pointed at her while the other man walked around our house.

At this point I was freaking out inside my bedroom, which was right by the living room. It seemed so unreal that I thought to myself, "Is this really happening?" My mind was going all over the place and I stupidly shut my door. As I shut the door one of the men called out that there was someone in the back room. My mother immediately had a mother instinct and told them it was her daughter and to leave me alone. She told them they could do whatever they wanted to her but to please leave her daughter alone. I was sitting on the floor at this time for no particular reason, and then all of a sudden I saw what looked like a combat boot appear from behind my room door to tell me to stay in my room and be quiet. I responded, "Yeah okay!" Then I heard my mother being told to go into the bathroom and shut the door. She did not move right away so one of the men yelled again for her to go into the bathroom. My door was shut so I was not aware of what was actually going on. After about five minutes my door suddenly swung opened and there stood my mother in front of me with no one around her. As she stood there looking at me, she asked if I was okay and if that had just really happened or had she just dreamt it.

Ten minutes later we had about half the police officers of Sioux Falls and Augustana Campus Security in our front yard. The police showed up quickly because a family friend who had been living with us in the basement called 911. My mother had never gotten the opportunity to call 911 before the men took my cell phone from her. The three of us were all questioned separately as to what had happened. Our family friend and I were not able to tell them much because my mother was the one who had the most contact with them. All three of us were in so much shock that we could see each other shaking. There is nothing that can describe that helpless feeling. We told the police if they had only gotten there a little sooner, they could have caught them. The main police officer remarked, "If we had gotten here any sooner, this whole situation could have gotten a lot worse for all of you. There is no way four men would have come walking nicely out of your house without a fight. Them having a gun would not have helped the situation either." My mother laughed and commented, "Yes, I never thought of it that way." She also asked if this happens a lot in Sioux Falls. They answered, "Breaking into houses yes, but not when people are also in the house at the same time." My mother also asked, "Isn't it pretty uncommon to bring a gun into a situation like this and not use it?" The police agreed with her. Luckily, for our sake, the gun was not used.

For a couple of years after that incident, my mother and I slept very uneasily and often had strong feelings of fear at night. When the sun would start setting we would get an anxious feeling deep in the pit of our stomachs. We joked with each other that if the sun would never set again we would never have that gnawing feeling. Because of what had happened that night, we changed many of our normal evening habits. We were always home before dark and always kept our living room lights and our television on while we slept. This was because when the four men broke in to our house it was pitch dark in the living room so it made it difficult when describing the four men to the police. My mother was only able to see their camouflage dress because of a street lamp across the road shining into our living room. My mother said only when the man with the gun turned to look at another one of the men did she realize there was a gun. The street lamp reflected the shiny silver of the rifle. This incident changed me deeply in that I recognize that with my size there would not be a way for me to actually even put up a fight if someone were to try to hurt me. I am even embarrassed to say that I started sleeping on the floor of my mother's bedroom because of my fear. We became prisoners in our own home at night for a very long time. I never wanted to stay home alone while my mother had meetings at night. Besides the men stealing my cell phone and my mother's purse they stole our feeling of security and their breaking into our home gave us an immense feeling of vulnerability.

Many people told us to move and find another place to rent until our house sold, but we did not. My mother explained to people that she and I had to work through our fears about the incident. She believed that running away from what happened would not help us at all. It was not an easy thing to do, but we did it. What helped us was that we bought a puppy a few months later and he needed to be walked. Walking him forced us to have to step outside during the night. We never ventured very far from the house with him, as we went for our walks at night. Another large part of losing our uneasiness was when my mother bought a new house. For me, leaving the little house by campus helped me resolve my fear issues, but not all of them. I still to this day do not answer the door when I am home alone unless I know ahead of time someone is coming over. Our friends and family members know to call me when they get close to our place before ringing the doorbell or knocking. Sometimes when I am home alone and hear something outside or my dog starts barking randomly, my heart starts to race and beat extremely fast. At that point I try to talk myself through the situation. I am always embarrassed that I start freaking out, and I find myself asking, "Where could I hide if I need to?" I know wherever I live throughout my life that the feeling of nervousness will more than likely never leave me whenever I am alone. On the other hand, life is all about working through unpleasant obstacles so that we all can deeply enjoy and appreciate the excellent parts of life.

The bottom line is that this whole incident made my mother and I very aware that if someone wants to get into our house, they can, unfortunately, achieve it. Having your house broken into can happen to anyone, anywhere. We lived in Vermillion for twenty years and never locked the door and were never broken into. My mother and I would have never dreamt that this could have ever happen to us. My message is that you can never be too careful with locking doors and windows. The only thing we can do is to make it intensely challenging for them to get into the house so that there is time to call 911. Then hopefully the person trying to get into the house would hear the sirens and start running away before anyone gets hurt. We were extremely fortunate with our outcome, which could have easily ended horribly. This situation only has to happen once to change someone's life forever. Once again, it was clear to us that God was at our side.

Experiencing the break-in profoundly changed me and encouraged me to take note of my surroundings when I am alone at night. Even though this was a terrifying experience the positive outlook on it is that my mother and I worked through our fears even though there were times we did not think we could. The absurd thing is that it is a great story to tell others now that years have passed. Many people are surprised and amazed when we tell them our story, because we are the last ones that people would have ever thought would have a home broken into. It just confirms that it does not matter who anyone is, break-ins can happen to anybody. As the years have gone by we have never forgotten that it happened, but we also try to not let it destroy our ability to move forward toward the future. The truth is, you are only as vulnerable as you let yourself be, and even though this experience was awful, both my mother and I are working hard to make it just another experience in our lives rather than something that controls us forever. We've learned from it and we are now doing what we can to learn from it and make lemonade from those very sour lemons.

Worries in the OR

My eyes begin to fill up with panicked tears,
As I can sense the whole room's anxious fears.
Doctors and nurses surround me; all they want to do is aid,
But can't go any further before the next step is heavily weighed.

I keep repeating with tears streaming down, "I am so sorry.
    I wish my gagging would end."
Above me I hear, "It's alright. You're going through a lot
    and we all want to commend."
Laying on the OR table I'm thinking, "Help me through this
    God, I trust you with all my might!"
A feeling of calmness comes over me as I know my Angel,
    Julie, is in sight.

Spinal surgery was a success and now all I have to
    do is wait to heal,
But as I reflect on what I have been through, it
    feels so surreal.
Regaining all the ground in which I have lost will
    take a lot of persistence,
But it is nothing I can't overcome – I know I
    can go the distance.

Written March 2009

Chapter 10

"All you have to do
is know where you're going.
The answers will come to you
of their own accord."
-Earl Nightingale

Using Technology to Fill the Void

Computers, Cell Phones and Constant Innovation

I grew up in an age when computers were not a common household item. The idea of having a computer for each individual within the household was not even a thought that crossed anyone's mind. If a friend had a computer, it was the coolest thing ever. It reminds me of the stories I have heard from my mother about when she would visit a friend or relative who had a color TV. In my adolescent days computers were so expensive to purchase that families put a lot of thought into buying one. I was in fourth grade when my family bought our first computer. It was an Apple Macintosh with dial-up internet. I still chuckle when I think about the whole dial-up internet phase of life. Children my age grew up listening to the little high and low pitched shrieks and sounds as our computer modems tried to connect to the World Wide Web, unlike today's children who just jump on the internet at any given time without waiting. With Wi-Fi they can also receive a connection to internet almost anywhere they go.

The same goes for growing up in the analog-only age of cell phones, where we actually had to remember people's phone numbers to call them. My first cell phone that I received was when I was in middle school. My mother and father bought it for me in case there was an emergency throughout the day. Those were the days that families typically only had one cell phone for a whole family. Since cell phones were not a common household item back then, it was pretty awesome to have one. Those cell phones were unlike present day cell phones; they were only to be used in case of emergencies, not like they are used now, every minute of every day.

I never wanted school rules to be broken for me because of my disability, but at times rules were bent to accommodate me. The rule in middle school was that our cell phones were supposed to be stored in our locker at all time. Since my cell phone was for emergencies during the school day I was allowed to keep mine in my purse. The worry was that there might have been a day where I could have gotten stuck in a room with no one around me to help me get to where I needed to be. Rule following has always been extremely important to me in life, so in middle school I never took my cell phone out of my purse if not necessary. I had my parents and schoolteachers' trust to act responsibly with my cell phone and I did not want to break that trust. While I'm fortunate to say that I never needed my cell phone in an emergency situation during middle school or high school, I cannot say the same for college. During my final year at Augustana College we had a terribly snowy winter and as I was traveling across campus one of my wheelchair wheels got stuck in a snowdrift. It was pretty humorous to me as I sat there realizing what had just happened. I pulled out my Blackberry and made a call for help, which arrived soon after. Thank goodness for ever-improving modern technology. With today's social media networking platforms I can update my Facebook status, Tweet, and blog all at the same time while I wait for help if it ever happens again!

I have seen many technological innovations such as computers, internet, and cell phones improve as each year goes by. Through these technological innovations I have been able to overcome some of the difficulties of transportation. Instead of driving to a friend's home, I can instant message, text, or Skype. If I cannot get to work one day, I can still get on the web and find resources to send out to people. Technology such as blogging, Twitter, Facebook, YouTube, and Skype have assisted me in beginning the process of accomplishing the numerous goals I have set for my life. In addition to those technologies helping me, a cell phone with internet access doubles as a mobile office, meaning I am only one click away from what I need to do and one click away from knowing what is going on in the world.

Spreading the Word Worldwide

By utilizing these various technologies and social media tools, I am able to move toward my goal of assisting families and children who have Mucopolysaccharidosis or any other medical condition. Each of these social media platforms provides different avenues for sharing my message with others. They allow me to encourage people to live life to the fullest and not worry so much about what we cannot do or how we might lack certain abilities, because the truth of the matter is that everyone has to deal with some sort of challenge or obstacle. It is all a part of something we call life.

I have created a video entitled *Living with MPS VI.* I did this hoping that others who have MPS or have someone in their family who has MPS can see that life with MPS has difficulties, but that does not mean individuals should give up on themselves in life. After finalizing this video I uploaded it on my personal Facebook page and a Facebook page I created called *MPS Awareness.* I also uploaded it to YouTube for others to view. Following my upload to the Facebook page *MPS Awareness*, I received a wonderful comment from a mother who has a daughter with MPS. She wrote,

> "Kendra, this is without a doubt the most inspiring thing I have ever seen. You deserve enormous credit for it. I'm incredibly grateful that I got to see it, and I came upon it at a very good time. Just when I was having a down day, worrying about my daughter, I see you in that slideshow - not just smiling, but beaming the whole way through your years, and I honestly think it's the most wonderful thing. Thank you so much for sharing this with us, you've given me some hope. I am genuinely in awe."

Numerous others have shared similar remarks about seeing me smile all the way through the video. I was surprised that so many commented on that because I have watched it many times and have never really noticed me constantly smiling. Later I saw that another woman had shared my video on her personal Facebook page, and she added a note with it: "This is a woman that has the same illness as my Granddaughters Makenzie and Isabella! This shows just what children with MPS can do in their life! Very Proud of You Kendra." Comments like these make me even more passionate about spreading my message of hope and staying positive throughout life's challenges.

If you want to see the video, you can search for "Living with MPS VI" on YouTube or you can scan the QR code included here with a QR code scanner and pull it up on your smartphone:

Part of my desire to reach out to families and individuals dealing with MPS VI inspired me to get involved on social networks. As of now, I'm active on both my personal blog and on Twitter. I am still getting the hang of both networks. The blog I created is *Kendra's Catchy Korner* and my Twitter name is @Kegottsleben. These two social media networks will help me work toward my goal of spreading my message of hope to others. I use my blog to share my thoughts, describe various incidents I've gone through and how I worked through each, sharing positive quotes I like and talking about things I generally just ponder about in life. I love using Twitter to respond to people I see talking about hardships due to MPS, disabilities, and other medical conditions. I also use both as a forum to simply show that I can live a normal, happy life even if I have a disability of some sort. I have a lot of room for growth within these two social networking mediums to become more efficient in placing my individual stamp.

I've also been able to interact on a deeper, more personal level with a wide variety of people through my Facebook page. Some of my favorite online conversations have taken place with people who write on my wall or whose walls I visit and leave comments on. Beyond sharing positive growth experiences throughout my life, I regularly post positive quotes from famous and non-famous individuals. These quotes always get a good number of "Likes" and comments from people who appreciate a boost of positivity. Keeping an optimistic mindset is one of the best ways to make sure things fall into place in a positive way at the right time, and I'm thankful I am able to do that through Facebook, Twitter and my blog.

Another tool I have started using is Skype, which allows me to converse face-to-face with others across the United States. Skype provides an opportunity for traditional face-to-face interaction to occur with others no matter how far away the individuals actually are. I have Skyped with a friend from West Virginia and one from New Orleans as well as relatives in Maryland, Florida and even Washington. I am still amazed at how the whole Skyping concept works. Skype is another tool that I have as a form of communication, but I haven't used it on a regular basis. I am looking forward to using it much more as I begin to get my message of hope out to others, making the distance of spreading the word face-to-face unstoppable no matter where I am.

The Advantages of Social Networking

Technology gives us the ability to not be judged by our physical appearances, but rather just on our words and personality traits. These technology tools have assisted me in becoming more independent throughout my life. They allow me the capability of getting my message out to others in the global world without having to constantly travel. As technology has grown, so has my ability to expand my networks. I have been able to make many new connections with others, especially within the MPS community. I have had the opportunity, through Facebook, to develop a friendship with a woman around my age from Norway. What is so fascinating with this connection is that she also has MPS VI. Without Facebook I may have never had the chance to widen my friendship span all the way to Norway. These technologies have made it accessible for me in discussing and assisting others from my computer with the help of internet and social media tools.

I would seriously recommend other individuals in my similar situation to start using social networking platforms for making connections with others. These tools allow your voice to be easily heard from one continent to another. Being able to connect online dismisses the barriers of size, ability and physical maneuvering. It is not always easy to find people nearby who can understand or relate to what someone else is going through, such as

MPS patients, for example. These social media and networking tools can improve that dilemma. It is amazing how far away people can be while still sharing enlightening and inspiring conversations. I know I have had such conversations on numerous occasions.

A perfect example of being able to connect with someone from across the world at a pivotal point in another's life without realizing the impact was the time I sent a "South Dakota is still extremely proud of you," message to Derek Miles. He is a former University of South Dakota pole vault athlete, who placed fourth in the 2008 Olympic Games. When I sent my encouraging message full of heartfelt support, I had no expectation of receiving a message back. So, when I saw his name pop up in my e-mail listings and read his response, I realized how my gesture of support made a difference for him. I had expressed how I understood how disappointing it must have been being so close to reaching his dream of winning an Olympic medal, but that I and many others were still tremendously proud of him for what he had achieved. It takes tough work and dedication to get to the Olympics, and he did it, even though the result did not come out the way he would have liked. He e-mailed me back a message of gratitude for sending a best of luck message.

A few days later my father sent me an e-mail telling me of a site where Derek had been blogging throughout his whole experience during the 2008 Olympics. My father had added in the subject line of the e-mail "Derek mentioned you in his blog." That was really exciting for me to see what he had written. His blog read…"After the competition, I returned to the village fairly disappointed and continued to stew until morning. When I awoke, I turned on my phone, which promptly registered multiple e-mails of cybernetic pats on the back. One in particular came from Kendra Gottsleben, the daughter of USD men's track coach Dave Gottsleben. Kendra is an amazing individual who has battled life with a flame far greater than the Olympic torch I competed under. With limited mobility, she has taken life to greater places than I can ever hope to…" After reading Derek's blog I was impressed with his honesty about his feeling of frustration of being so close but yet so far away from the Olympic medal. I was also extremely flattered at his thoughtful words about me. In addition to Derek Miles being a great athlete he is an extremely wonderful individual and character.

I know that when I was diagnosed with Mucopolysaccharidosis Type VI there were not many places to find resources of information about MPS or places where my parents could learn more about what my future could possibly hold. Now with the internet and these social media networking tools, families, friends, and individuals who have a medical condition can benefit from all the information that is out there.

They can make connections with others who are going through the same types of life circumstances and become support networks for one another.

All in all, it is not the technology that matters most; it is the people behind the technology that really makes a difference. But being able to connect online has helped these same people share advice, encouragement and inspiration in ways that were not possible in years past, which makes me very excited to see where technology is able to take us in the future.

Chapter 11

"The only way of finding the limits of the possible
is by going beyond them into the impossible."
-Arthur C. Clarke

Making Choices

Think Before You Act

Life is all about making choices each and every day. What we decide to do is entirely up to us. All over the world people wake up daily and have the option to either have a day full of success or a day full of complaining, choosing to waste yet another beautiful day that God has given them. Of course, such as life goes, there will always be days that do not turn out to be what one might have hoped. When a day like that occurs, it is an opportune time to decide to not let that imperfect incident ruin the rest of the week or even let it affect the rest of the day. *You* have the ability to make the choice.

The decision to have a splendid day has only to do with one's personal perspective on life. I try to always see the positive in each situation, because we can always learn from incidents that happen to us and others as time goes on. Life is all about learning and being observant as to what is going on around us daily. Trust me when I say that I've had my share of moments when I had to search long and hard for the positive in a frustrating situation. Sometimes I do not end up seeing the positive immediately or even days after the incident. Occasionally, it has taken over a year or two to actually see what I gained from an unfortunate situation.

A perfect example is when one of my college professors told me she thought I took the easy way out, and that I was not graduate school material. In this occasion it took me about a week to realize the positive side of the situation – that she created a fire within me to prove her notion wrong. The professor's comments also made me take some time to reflect on myself and my ambitions in life, but I did come to the conclusion that I have accomplished a lot in my lifetime, and that I will not stop anytime soon. Someday I know that, should I choose to go on to graduate school, I will be able to face that challenge confidently, no matter what my professor may think.

With that in mind I try to not react instantaneously after each negative incident. Many times when someone immediately responds or judges quickly, things get much worse than they actually were in the first place. I once found myself in one of these predicaments, but I fortunately refrained from making any split-second response out of frustration, even though I felt as if I was being falsely accused. When I was a freshman in college I was accused of cheating on one of my first psychology exams. What had happened was that I had asked the secretary prior to beginning my exam if it was acceptable to start an exam, give it to her if I was not finished, and then come back and finish it after class. Her response was "Yes." So I began my test and then saw my time running short, so I handed it to her and left for class. When I arrived back to the secretary's office to finish, I was swiftly and inaccurately accused of cheating on my test by another Augustana faculty member. When I was confronted, I was so caught off guard by this accusation that I did not really know how to react other than wanting to burst into tears and begin to start pointing fingers at the secretary, but I did not. As I sat and listened to how what I had just done was unacceptable and was not what Augustana stood for, I made the choice to not act on my feeling of irritation, aggravation, and humiliation. Later that week I retook the exam and discussed the issue calmly. I explained that I was unaware of the rule and if I had been made aware of it when I first started college it would not have happened. I also explained that, now that I knew the rule, this situation would never come up again. Eventually, an agreement was reached for future test taking that worked well for everyone. In these types of circumstances it's important that you not react (or *overreact*) immediately without taking some time to put your thoughts together. Stepping back and reflecting on what happened later when you're more relaxed will allow you to think much more clearly. As those situations happen to me, I always try and tell myself that there are too many hours in the day to let several minutes destroy a whole day that God has given me.

The Path We Take

If we want to achieve our dreams and goals, we have to be creative and inventive as we try to make them come true. For the most part, dreams and goals do not come true by others just handing them to us or just sitting around doing nothing. Accomplishing the goals that we have set for ourselves will only happen if we decide to start down the path of attainment. The actual steps that it takes to reach our aspirations are all a part of the larger journey of life. We as individuals grow within ourselves and outwardly through each step we take toward our goals. After fulfilling those ambitions, there is a much greater sense of satisfaction as you look back at where you started and see where you finally ended up. Sometimes the route we think we are going to take is not the actual route we travel. We have to recognize the critical times when we may need to make slight alterations to the route we're taking to achieve our ambitions. Those minor adjustments are usually what make the difference in reaching our final destination. When someone is handed their dreams and goals on a silver platter, they are more apt to not be as passionate about them, because there was not much effort used to reach their aims. Such individuals are not used to having to actually work rigorously for their ultimate goal. Even though it takes a lot of diligent work in obtaining our dreams, it does not mean it is impossible. As long as people set their mind to something they want to accomplish, anything is possible. In life, there is an unlimited amount of potential for each one of us every day. We are the ones who have to make it happen for ourselves.

Making a Difference

There are countless people in today's society that not only have a positive outlook on life but have also decided to try and make a difference and make their own individual mark on the world. I know that I try to do this every day in my daily experiences. There are many people who may think that making a difference is too difficult to do, but it really is not. Simply smiling or saying "Hi" to another person passing by on the sidewalk can make a huge impact. You may not know how much you could do for someone else with an effortless gesture. I know when someone says "Hi" to me or smiles as I pass them, I cannot help but return a smile. It always makes my day a lot brighter. It is part of being human to enjoy being acknowledged by others. I have had conversations with people who have tended to be a bit negative about life, and one thing they have mentioned was that no one ever took the time to acknowledge that they even existed. Even taking the time to talk to a friend, family member, or anyone in need of a meaningful conversation can influence someone's day immensely. Maybe a friend needs a ride to a job interview and, rather than making them wait on an unreliable bus or taxi, you help ensure that the friend arrives a few minutes early to the interview. That early arrival could be the determining factor between the person being offered the job or not, all because you took the time to help.

Everyone has crosses to bear that may not be easily seen, and just being genuinely warm-hearted, compassionate, and thoughtful toward another individual is a way of positively shaping what goes on in the world. The movie *Pay It Forward*, released in 2000, follows along with this notion. Even though the main character is met with tragedy while trying to "pay it forward" for a fellow schoolmate, he never backed down. He was just a little boy who made his impact on a community and forever changed the idea of "paying it forward." On a smaller scale of "paying it forward," one individual smiles and says "Hi" to another and then that next person interacts with someone else positively. It starts to develop into a chain reaction. People like to pass on pleasant vibes toward one another no matter who they are after receiving some themselves. No matter how monumental or minuscule the gesture, it has the power to shape everyone's interactions in one way or another within society.

One way I intend to "pay it forward" is by helping others who have physical disabilities. I have been asked many times what advice I would give other individuals my age that either have MPS VI or are in a wheelchair on how to keep a positive attitude throughout life. My first response is that just because people have to deal with obstacles does not mean that they as individuals have to let that define who they actually are as a person. I know that I do not let my struggles define me. I was born just plain "Kendra Gottsleben" way before I was ever diagnosed with my health condition, and that has been the attitude I have lived with ever since. I also think that it is extremely important for everyone to understand that life is filled with all kinds of challenges for each of us. Everything we experience, no matter what it is, will affect us in some way, shape, or form. I am not a believer in letting my heath condition limit everything I want to pursue in life. When I look at what I want out of life, I see that there is not much time for me to dwell on my limitations. Instead I concentrate on my abilities. The bottom line is that I will not stop being me just because there have been roadblocks throughout life. I have made the conscious decision each day to try and overcome the difficulties I have to face. I try to be seen as independent of my disability so that people see me for me. I know that I am not the only one who has this same notion about triumphing over their struggles. There are numerous others in society that make this choice throughout their lives. I have yet to see someone who has not had to deal with some type of hurdle during his or her lifetime.

Positive, but Realistic

While I may have the motivation to accomplish my dreams and goals, I am also a very matter-of-fact individual. I recognize there are things that are literally impossible for me to achieve. I know I will never be able to run a mile, win an award for being the best basketball player, or excel at any sport. But I acknowledge the gifts that I have been given, and those are what will lead me to success in my life. We have all been given gifts in our lives, and the process of identifying them is part of knowing oneself. We regularly discover new tidbits about ourselves from occurrences that happen during any given day. We actually never stop growing within ourselves, but as long as we have a strong foundation of our beliefs and values, we will be competent in life. I have told some individuals within the disability community to "Own their disabilities and not let their disabilities own them." At the same time, this message fits anyone in the world when you adjust the wording: "Own who you are; do not let your limitations own you." The sooner we truly know ourselves and what we stand for in life, the sooner we can be successful. Knowing ourselves means identifying all of our vulnerabilities, shortcomings, imperfections, excellent skills, special talents, and strengths as a person.

I have heard stories about people who have a disability and are not comfortable in their own skin, and sometimes this can lead to failure. For example, I have heard of college students who are dyslexic and do not want their peers to know of the disability, so they never tell the disability coordinator on campus. Then mid-term grades come out, and their grades are terrible. At that point there is not much that can be done because the professors were not made aware of the student's disability. The sooner someone owns his or her disability, the sooner others will see past it. Another example is a person who might not have a disability at all admitting to a co-worker that she or he is not familiar with a certain computer program but is very eager to learn. The ability to confidently ask for help allows her or him to own their lack of knowledge rather than letting it own them and cause problems down the line.

My Portacath Predicament

Sometimes a person has to make the hard choice to make life a little easier. For over a year I woke up one day a week with an uneasy and nervous feeling in the pit of my stomach, as a result of my weekly trips to receive my infusion at what was then the Sioux Valley Children's Specialty Clinic. My medical condition has a tendency to give nurses, doctors, lab technicians, and anesthesiologists the difficult challenge of inserting intravenous lines (aka IVs) in my veins. More times than I would like to remember, I left the clinic with numerous colorful Band-Aids due to their inability to get the IV inserted correctly the first, second, third (fourth, fifth, sixth…) time. Realizing those weekly visits were never going to stop for the rest of my life, my nurses and doctor started talking to me about receiving a portacath.

The day I was strongly advised to consider receiving a portacath from the medical staff started out as a rough morning, needle-wise. It was without a doubt the longest time I had ever gone without any of the needles staying in my veins like they were supposed to. This particular morning my veins were especially uncooperative. I stopped counting how many times I had been poked after the eighteenth poke (and I'm not exaggerating). After two hours of poking every vein from my arms to my toes, calling in the flight crew who were trained to get IVs inserted in emergency situations, and then bringing in an anesthesiologist just to get one IV in, I knew it was time to do something.

My nurses, Nancy and Dawn, told me that they wanted Carrie, the Child Life Specialist, to show me what one looked like and how it would work within my body. Carrie explained to me that a portacath was a little medical device that would be inserted beneath my skin either around my upper chest area or just below my clavicle or collarbone. She said when inserted, the portacath is surgically attached to a vein within my body. The portacath has a septum that permits drugs to be injected and blood samples to be drawn countless times. This would allow me to have less pain, rather than being stuck each week numerous times with sharp needles that did not stay in. Carrie expressed to me that portacaths are mostly implanted into people who have to be poked more often than the average person. Many such individuals are hematology and oncology patients. Knowing that I was going to have to have this treatment weekly for the rest of my life, I was also a good candidate.

I completely understood their reasoning for me to receive the portacath, and it really was not the actual device being inside my body that concerned me; it was what I was going to have to actually go through to have it inserted in me. I knew that the surgery would not be a simple surgery; it would be a complicated procedure. I was mostly apprehensive about the process of intubation, because I know that I am extremely difficult to intubate. I was frightened that something terrible might happen to me during the surgery. Nancy and Dawn recognized my concerns and remarked, "Kendra, going through this type of situation every week is exhausting you both physically and emotionally! You're a strong person who can make it through the surgery just fine." So, we made an appointment with the University of Minnesota Medical Center, Fairview in Minneapolis, Minnesota.

As my parents and I arrived at the University of Minnesota Medical Center, Fairview we met with a nurse named Carol. We met with her because the doctor was busy with another surgery at that time. I was a little nervous, because I wanted to know someone who would be in the operating room the next day. I decided to ask Carol if she was going to be in the operating room with me. Sadly, her response was, "No, I have nothing to do with the operating room scene anymore; I just do the doctor's paperwork and talk to patients."

That did not ease my feelings of apprehension at all. Because the doctor knew of my intubation challenges, he had decided to do the surgery with me under a local anesthetic, which is similar to when someone gets their teeth drilled on and given Novocain medicine. That meant I was going to be awake throughout the procedure. That is why I wanted to be familiar with someone who was going to be in the operating room. I have always gotten a kick out of it when on the operating table doctors say to me, "Kendra, do you remember me?" and I always want to say, "Um, sorry, but no! You have a mask on your face, and all I can see are your eyes!" I asked Carol a few questions like how long the surgery would last, whether or not I'd feel a lot of pain during and after, and how long I would be sore following surgery. She answered all of my questions as best as she could. Talking about what would be going on in the operating room during my surgery definitely helped to ease my fears, but I still wasn't exactly feeling cheery about everything either.

As my parents and I were leaving the office, Carol told us she decided that she would scrub in the next day for my surgery so that I could at least recognize someone in there. I breathed a sigh of relief. "Thank goodness, I will know at least one person in there with me," I thought. That made me smile so wide that my little crooked teeth showed. I felt so much better after she said she would be with me. I knew having her there would help me to not think about the doctor cutting me open and putting a foreign device inside me. I think she knew that I was mostly scared about being awake, and she was right. I have been sent many angels in my life, and I believe that she was one of them. Carol knew that I had experienced many surgeries, but never while being awake. From her numerous surgeries she had attended, she must have been motivated to assist me because she realized that having someone to be able to talk to throughout the ordeal would be greatly beneficial.

The next day, I went to the hospital at 6:30 a.m. and checked in. My parents and I then went back to the waiting room. I put on a stunning, beauty pageant-worthy hospital gown, while the doctor talked to my mother and father. He came in to talk to me and ran through everything once again, before whisking me away. It took a long time with the doctor's detail discussion, and I had huge butterflies in my stomach the whole time! My mother and father were quiet while we were waiting for me to go into surgery. They played it tough for me, even though they wanted to grab me and run in the opposite direction of the operating room. I know they did not want me to worry; they wanted me to be strong. I was strong for them, and they were strong for me, even though I knew they were scared out of their minds for me.

The doctor finally said it was time to go and started rolling me away. That is always a very miserable and terrifying time for me. I saw my mother get teary eyed as she said she loved me and would be waiting for me. Then I looked into my father's eyes, which were filled with great sadness and concern. As I was rolled away, I saw them getting farther and farther away from me. It never gets any easier for them or me. At the time of our goodbyes, before each surgery, there is always this unspeakable look of hope from both of their faces that the next time they see me they pray that I am alive. It hurts me every time I have to put them through that kind of torture. Parents never want to see a child of theirs in any sort of pain, and my parents are certainly no different.

My nerves started to settle down little by little as I entered the operating room. The doctor came over and put an IV in my arm. Ironically, even he had to poke me two times to get an IV in. The IV helped me a great deal, because he put the local anesthetic medicine in the tubing, which relaxed me. My nerves dwindled down after a couple of minutes as the medicine began running through my body. It worked like a charm.

After the IV was in, nurses put numerous warm blankets all around me. It was a pretty strange experience for me, because I was awake and fully aware the whole time. They put a little blue tarp between my chest and my chin, so I could not see what was going on. They did some more prepping and then the doctor told me he was going to begin. I gave a sluggish smile and an all clear to go. During the entire procedure, the doctor talked to me. It was so surreal. He made sure I knew what was going on at all times. Carol stood near my head the whole time, and answered all the questions I had.

What was so fascinating to me during surgery was what the doctor and nurses actually talked about throughout the surgery. It was kind of like what you see on television. They discussed what was going on in their own lives, or what had happened to them recently that day. Before that surgery I thought that the television shows were exaggerating about what was discussed in the operating room. I thought that there would be more medical terminology used. It was humorous, but it was comforting at the same time, because the conversations made it not so scary. They kept me comfortable and did not talk about every last detail of what was actually occurring during the procedure.

About two and a half hours later, after the surgery was completed, Carol rolled me into the recovery room. She explained to me I would have to stay in the recovery room for three hours until I was able to go home. Carol then quickly disappeared into the hall to retrieve my parents from the waiting room. I was extremely groggy, so I did not communicate much with my parents when they came in. I just felt I needed to close my eyes and rest.

Of course my mother and father wanted to know how it was being awake during the surgery. I informed them it was not as tough and terrifying as I thought it would be. I explained how the doctor and nurses conversed as if they were at a coffeehouse or talking on the street with friends. They thought that the conversations that occurred were pretty amusing too.

After about three hours of laying in the recovery room I was ready to leave and head home. As I was changing back into my clothes, I winced as I felt a sharp shooting pain travel from my arm to my chest. I was not expecting such pain. A recovery nurse saw me wince and said I was going to be in pain for a while and handed me an ice pack. She added that I could take some Advil if I so desired, but I opted not to. I have never really liked taking pills. I was surprised by how much relief the ice pack provided for lessening the pain. I knew I could manage as long as I did not move much.

When it was all said and done, I realized that the portacath was probably the best thing I had ever received! It was a life-changing decision. It has only taken one poke each week for my IVs since I got it. I love the portacath, and so do my nurses, Nancy and Dawn. I do contemplate about the day I will have to replace it, but I have determined I will cross that bridge when that time comes. Having the portacath has made my being poked, stress free. It still hurts, but not as much as it did when I was being poked numerous times. I am glad that I have it, and that it is not very noticeable. Most importantly, I learned from this experience that sometimes, no matter how scary the "harder" choice may seem, it can end up being the better option in the long run.

Sometimes we tend to avoid situations or other life circumstances that we do not want to deal with, but in the end they turn out to be the best thing for us. We have to decide to work through those situations so that they make us stronger for others who will enter our lives in the future. Life is all about overcoming challenges and not running away from them when they appear. Dealing with challenges head on is, in my opinion, the best way to achieve success in all circumstances.

<u>Incapable vs. Capable</u>
Looking at me what do you see?
My lack of physical ability,
Or my positive upbeat smile?

My hope is at that all you truly see is me.
Being disabled is not my entire reality.
I don't let myself be limited—all the while.

Making the best of what life has given me is my aim.
Feelings of remorsefulness towards me—are unnecessary.
My challenges have shaped me into the person you see today.

Life has its ups and downs; that is part of the
truthfulness of the game.
Similar to everyone else I have dreams
—one in particular is to marry.
Giving up on life because of roadblocks in the
way is not me, for some it may.

Everyone has struggles in life; it doesn't matter who
they are or what they look like.
No one is absolutely free from challenges, some are
visible and some are invisible.
Happiness for all the blessings received throughout
my life is what I always try to remember.

Written March 2009

Chapter 12

*"Never believe that a few caring people
can't change the world.
For, indeed, that's all who ever have."*
-Margaret Mead

Appreciating the "Little" Things in Life

Capable Kendra

As an Augustana College graduate with a double major in sociology and psychology, I am not that surprised to hear from others that I am exceptionally good at making people feel comfortable around me. I am always glad to hear that comment, because I never want anyone to feel sorry for me or feel like they cannot talk to me. I recognize that I have great empathy for others no matter what their life experiences are. Because I am limited in my physical abilities, I am always pleased when I am able to assist any of my friends or family members with the insight and understanding I have developed over the years. The sense of happiness that comes over me results from my feeling that I have made someone else's day brighter and better. Over time, I have developed an ability to be both an exceptional listener and someone who has a tendency to be nonjudgmental. I know how wonderful it is to have someone listen to me when I am in need of guidance and support, which is one of the many reasons I truly enjoy being there for anyone who needs someone to confide in. I've made it a personal mission to be helpful and supportive for others.

I realize that my positive perspective toward life may appear incredible to others who do not know me well and are seeing my cover rather than the pages on the inside, but my life really is not that remarkable. I am just a determined person like countless others. I do not see myself as being that much different from anyone else in my peer group, other than having a few...unique...challenges in my life. However, there are still times when I appreciate the little things in life that the average person may not stop to think about.

It may seem silly, but opening doors is one of those wonderful little gestures I appreciate that can make my day significantly easier. I am a person who always—and I do mean always—says "Thank you" whenever someone opens a door for me. I do not get upset when people do not open doors for me, because I don't expect them to. I also acknowledge that they are not purposely trying to be unhelpful to me. There are many circumstances that might cause people to not be helpful; they may be in a major rush, or they may not have even seen me (remember, I am *really* short). I am not the type of person who expects people to cater to my needs because I am in a wheelchair and only three feet tall. It's always a blessing when someone does decide to open a door for me.

As a woman in my late twenties, I really appreciate others who treat me as a fellow peer in my age group. One of the most wonderful compliments I receive from other people is that they do not see my disability, but rather they see me as an individual first. I have had many friends see past my disability to the point that they completely forget that I am extremely short. They are so used to me that when they are talking to others about me they never use the words "short," "in a wheelchair" or "has MPS." Not until after someone who does not know me well says, "Is that the friend you were telling me about? Wow, she is *really* short," my friends respond with something like, "Oh, yeah…I guess you could say that." The acceptance from others as "Kendra Gottsleben" rather than "Kendra Gottsleben, who has MPS VI and is in a wheelchair" is what reminds me each time of how important it is to have people see *me* first and my disability second.

My cousins on both sides of my family are also people in my life that have always seen past my physical limitations. I have never felt as though they pitied me, no matter what age we were.

They picked on me like they would any cousin whom they love, and I did the same to them. My cousins have always treated me like there is no difference between me and them. Of course they have helped me by giving me a hand here and there, but it never seemed like a big deal to them. What I love about my younger cousins is that, despite our differences, they still look to me for advice. I was not sure as I grew up if my younger cousins would be able to see past my inabilities so that we maintain a tight connection. Many of my cousins and I have such close-knit relationships, it's as if we are brothers and sisters. I have an especially close relationship with my cousin Erinn now that she lives in the same town as I do. I look forward to being a part of her life as a cousin/sister as she continues growing into a mature, beautiful, and remarkable young lady. If the various stories and memories I have shared in this book have not made it obvious by now, family is very important to me.

I have never seen myself as being different from my friends or cousins, other than my stature. But over time, as I realized individuals within the community were also actually recognizing me, as "Kendra Gottsleben," I began to realize I truly could do anything I wanted to in life. All through my life, especially middle school, high school, and college, I have never wanted others to see me as incapable, but rather capable, and I have proudly achieved that.

Traveling Toward Independence

While I know other individuals in our society use physical fitness or academic pursuits as useful ways to handle stressors in life or as an outlet to gain a better perspective on life's situations, I instead have chosen the creativity route. Painting, drawing, designing on computers, writing stories, and writing poetry are my ways of releasing stress. These artistic methods of expressing myself are skills that have guided me to a better perspective on life countless times. I can easily entertain myself for hours when I immerse myself in one of these outlets. I know that my imaginative ability is another form of freedom for me. I can convey my hopes, dreams, goals, and desires for myself through them. I truly appreciate my ability to be creative and I'm thankful to have the freedom to be myself in any situation. I have never had the feeling that I am less than others because of the cards I've been dealt throughout my life, and a big part of that is the fact that, no matter what my circumstances are, my creativity lets me do anything I can imagine. If I were to feel ashamed of who I am and what I have had to go through in life, I would not have made it as far as I have. My creativity has helped me become the proud, confident person I am today.

At the age of 23, as a soon-to-be senior in college, I was extremely proud of myself after attending my first MPS VI Conference in Vancouver, BC. I was invited by the pharmaceutical company to serve on a Patient Advisory Board to represent MPS VI patients receiving the enzyme replacement drug. The conference was designed mainly to discuss the impact MPS VI has had on my life and other participants. As I reflected on my life shortly after that trip, I clearly saw the path that led me to my position on the Patient Advisory Board, and what I had done with my life up to that point. After my trip, I came back with a new type of excitement for my future and all of my possibilities. I had always hoped to make a difference in the world, and I believe that this trip helped me to see that I was achieving my goal.

The trip that summer was just the beginning of a summer of growth for me. I traveled to Vancouver, BC, with my Aunt Denise and Uncle Loren, which marked the first time that I had ever traveled that far without my mother. In addition to that, I traveled to an entirely different country without her (and all of the troubleshooting she typically provides). I needed to do much of the problem-solving myself. I gained more independence that summer than I could have ever imagined. My mother and I have been through many ups and downs during life together, as is often the case with best friends. She has always been there cheering, pushing, and supporting me to achieve all my ambitions. The MPS VI Conference was the first time I felt people saw me as an independent individual and not my mother *and* me as a team. It was difficult for me at first to not have her there, but I knew I could do it. She also knew I was capable of doing it alone. This was a pivotal point in my life. She had prepared me well, and I wanted to show everyone that I knew what I was talking about when I said I wanted to make the world a better place to live in. Little did I know what I was going to gain from the experience in Vancouver. I was getting closer to entering the "real world" of work soon, and that trip made me feel more confident about entering that big, wide world. Vancouver also helped me realize and see for the first time that I truly do have something to say – and that people are actually interested in hearing it!

Having Mucopolysaccharidosis Type VI can have its challenges, but it is what you do with those challenges that makes you who you are. No one knows what life has in store for him or her. One can only believe and trust that God has a plan for them; I believe and trust that is true for me. I could not have gotten to where I am today without Him. This is an ongoing way of life for me, praying to God to show me the road to travel. I have hopes and dreams for my future in life. This does not mean that I do not have doubts, but when those doubts arise, that is when I need to put my trust in God the most! And every time I have put my trust in God, he's led me to wonderful outcomes, like giving me opportunities to meet and help others with MPS.

Attending the MPS VI Conference gave me a great deal of confidence in myself. I was actually helping others learn about what I have and how I do not let my disability control my life. I love sharing my life with others and helping people understand that they do not have to feel sorry for me. I am actually quite happy with the way my life has turned out so far. Being positive is the key to how I try to live. My life motto is, after all, "When life hands you a lemon, make lemonade."

An M&M Freak

A very kind and older friend of my dad's, whom I called Papa Less, introduced me when I was only five years old to one of my longest-running true loves. This love was something that could cheer me up when I was blue and entertain me with all its bright colors. I became extremely fond of plain M&M's. Papa Less would always buy me a bag of M&M's while I sat watching my father play for the Smith Dodgers in softball games and tournaments during the summer months. He was my Grandpa in my hometown of Vermillion even though we were not blood-related. The candy was a huge treat that I always looked forward to as my parents and I headed to the games. Still to this day the plain milk chocolate M&M's are my favorite candy. My love for M&M's has grown into quite a collection of figurines, clothing, pictures, note cards, pens, stuffed pillows, etc. I could go on and on. It has been fun to always be on the watch for M&M memorabilia.

As long as I can remember, M&M's have been my chosen candy anywhere I have gone. My mother told me that when my hair stylist found out I enjoyed them, she began having them on hand for me to snack on while I received haircuts. Typically young children do not like to sit completely still for very long time—especially for haircuts—and apparently the M&M's did the trick to keep me busy while my hair stylist was doing her magic with my hair. I remember my mother telling me that she was not going to keep buying M&M collectables, because she said I was going to grow out of this phase. For better or worse, I still have not grown out of it. I am 27 years old and still enjoy M&M's memorabilia as much as I did as I child.

Just a few years ago I found that there were two stores in the United States that were filled with M&M's merchandise. Going to an M&M store was one of my silly aims. I had always wanted to see a store devoted to M&M's someday (come on…wouldn't you want to see an entire store dedicated to *your* favorite thing?). After my family members had planned a trip to New York City, I discovered that there was a third store opening in New York City's Times Square. Being the fanatic that I am about M&M's, I told my family that was a must see for me while on the trip to the Big Apple! The store was pretty incredible to me, but not to anyone else. My family humored me by saying they enjoyed it, but I know it was not one of their dreams to see a whole store dedicated to a type of candy. Of course, I hope someday to still see the other two stores as well. I am not saying the M&M's are the whole reason I have a positive attitude, but it is remarkable how seeing all the colors can make me smile no matter what. A happy life, in my opinion, means having magnificent colors that surround your environment. If someone were to ask anyone who knows me well about the whole M&M fascination they would say, "That's just Kendra; she's a bit of an M&M freak!"

Music, Camera, Action

There have always been many "little" things in life that have given me joy on a daily basis. Every day I find delight in using my creativity, visiting with others, and singing along with music while working or riding in the car. I appreciate all these "little" things because they keep life entertaining when life could otherwise be seen as boring. When I am asked to create a slideshow movie for someone, I get excited because that is when my creativity kicks into high gear. As I mentioned in a previous chapter, placing pictures and sometimes movie footage together with words and music is thrilling, as I let my mind go wild with possibilities. The music that is added to the movie is what makes the movie so powerful and moving. Choosing the songs is the most challenging part of the creative process, because I always try to fit the pictures with the best song possible.

There are two slideshows that I have created that I am extremely proud of. One of them is when I was asked by my father to create one for the University of South Dakota Track and Field "Alumni Meet" in 2005. He explained that his purpose for the movie was for it to be playing on the Jumbotron while the alumni ran around the track. I felt a little pressure after that, knowing it was going to be played on such a large scale, but knew I could do it. The movie illustrated 100 years of the USD Cross Country and Track and Field program. It was well-received by others who viewed it at the meet, and I was grateful. When I actually got to view my final product on the Jumbotron I could not stop smiling. As I sat there watching my creation play out, my mind traveled back to the memories of being a young child watching the screen at sporting events while scores were being updated and phrases like "Make Some Noise!" and " Go Yotes!" continually appeared on it. I had never imagined that I would someday create something that would be played on such a massive screen. I was honored that my father asked me to create it. I was even pleasantly surprised when one of the alumni athletes asked my father if I was majoring in graphic design while at college. My father replied that it was a hobby of mine. The alumnus was shocked and said "Well she has a knack for it!" and told my father to tell me to keep up the amazing work.

The second slideshow movie I am incredibly proud of was created for Grandpa Drew. He got the privilege to go on an Iowa Honor Flight to Washington, DC in June 2010 because he was a WWII veteran. He had already been to many of the amazing monuments before, since my Uncle Dan and his family lived out there for many years, but Grandpa was excited to be able to sightsee with fellow veterans like him. My family and I loved Grandpa so much that, without hesitation, we decided that we all wanted to surprise him and be there when he got off the plane returning from his trip. I collected the pictures and movie footage of us all welcoming him home and created a final product. Grandpa had no idea I was making him the movie, so when I showed him, he was speechless. I knew him too darn well and realized he was not saying much because he knew if he started to talk he would start crying. I wanted to share my movie with so many family and friends that I uploaded it to YouTube for others to see. I remember a day when Grandma Drew was talking to me on the phone and she told me that she'd had numerous people in town come up to her saying, "Jeanne that movie about Maurice's Honor Flight was amazing!" To my astonishment, the movie I had produced even brought tears to the eyes of people I did not even know. I did it all for Grandpa Drew. I cherish that movie so much because shortly after that wonderful Honor Flight trip he passed away. Losing him so abruptly made me thankful I was able to share my movie with him before he passed. In preparation for Grandpa's wake, my family decided to have two slideshow movies playing - the one the funeral home made and my Honor Flight slideshow movie.

Taking Time to Arm Dance

Along with my creativity, I greatly appreciate visiting with others wherever and whenever the opportunity arises. I have been told that I have an approachable way about me in many different situations. I am delighted that individuals feel that way about me. I definitely prefer to be asked a question rather than having people stare at me and wonder about me. I see myself as an open book and would love for others to see me that way too! I also enjoy conversing with others because I know how much visiting with someone, no matter the topic or situation, can be beneficial for everyone involved. Since a very young age, I have been referred to as a "little visitor." I have been found numerous times chatting with nurses, doctors, secretaries, and other employees while at my weekly infusions. I love talking with others because of what I can learn from simply talking to another person. The best way to become more aware about others who surround us in society is to take the time to listen and chat. Sometimes talking with others can be the best way to help a friend, coworker, or even a stranger to have a happier day.

I am appreciative of various "little" things in life, but in writing this book I realized how much music has motivated me in my life. Writing this book, for example, could not have been done without me listening to countless songs throughout the whole process. Even in high school and college I had to have tunes playing loudly to get my words onto the blank computer screen. I laughed at myself as I tried to write without listening to music. Nothing worth writing ever comes out. Music has a way of inspiring me to write sentences, then paragraphs, and finally pages. In addition to encouraging my writing process, I also greatly enjoy listening to the radio and my iPod in the car. In my family I am known as the "arm dancer." At one point in third and fourth grade I was in a dance academy program. I've always loved dancing ever since I was a child, but because I lack complete stability and energy while dancing, I have pretty much retired my dancing shoes to just "arm dancing." I still enjoy the thought of dancing and do miss that in life, but I make do with my "arm dancing."

Life needs to be about taking time to appreciate all the little and larger things that make us happy and successful in life. And in most cases, those little and large things have to do with other people. Whether saying thank you for opening the door, receiving a new M&M collectable, or making a slideshow for a loving relative, it is the personal connections that count the most. No one in our society can achieve their full potential without recognizing both types of acknowledgments, big and small. We cannot have one without the other. Appreciating the little things in life helps us aspire to reach our larger dreams and ambitions.

A Little Piece of Heaven

Brightly colored coating,
With a center full of flavor.

Simply creamy and smooth,
With no nuts in the middle.

Not crispy nor dark,
Not too big or too little.

Always stamped with the letter M,
Or sometimes a unique message.

"I love you" in red and white,
"It's a girl" in pink and purple.

They "Melt in your mouth,
Not in your hand."

The original,

The one and only...

PLAIN M&MS.

Written April 2009

Chapter 13

*"Life is a succession of lessons
which must be lived to be understood."
-Ralph Waldo Emerson*

Determination, Determination, Determination

Striving for the Best

I know that I have always been determined to pursue my ambitions no matter what. I set a goal to graduate from high school with a 3.5 grade point average and to do so as a member of the National Honor Society; both are goals that I accomplished. I even surpassed my initial goal by graduating with a 3.6. Of course, having a strong sense of determination does not make the actual process of trying to achieve success in your life an easy task. Like the saying goes, "No pain, no gain." It has taken a large amount of hard work and personal motivation to work toward my dreams and goals. Achieving the grade point average I worked for and becoming a member of National Honor Society were definitely challenging tasks, especially since, in the last two years of my high school career, I missed one day a week for my enzyme treatment. I am proud that I was never given a grade because of my life circumstances. I earned the grades I received because I worked hard for each and every one of them, and I wouldn't have wanted it any other way.

Each one of us needs motivation and a strong work ethic to reach *any* of our goals. For example, Olympic athletes do not attain their success without willpower and the passion to achieve maximum potential. I have gotten to personally watch Derek Miles, an Olympic pole vaulter, grow from his college days at the University of South Dakota to participating in the Olympics. His determination is something to admire. Many people have achieved success in their lives, but each and every person has had to work tremendously hard to attain their dreams and goals. As humans, roadblocks appear at different times on our path towards success. That is just the way life goes. The sooner we accept that challenges are going to spring up unexpectedly throughout life, the sooner we can focus on overcoming those challenges.

Finding Success Amidst Doubt

Numerous people have told me that they did not think I could accomplish certain feats during my lifetime. Through hard work and motivation, I proved them wrong and rose above many of those challenges. I enjoyed proving wrong my high school counselor who didn't think I was college material. It took me six full years to complete college, but I did receive a bachelor's degree with a double major in sociology and psychology. It took me six full years because, as a result of my weekly infusion treatments and the various challenges they would present, I had decided to take only nine credits each semester rather than a "full" schedule (though I can assure you that my schedule still felt plenty "full" even with just those nine credits). Graduating from college would not have been possible without a great deal of determination, a passion for what I was doing, and a belief that I could accomplish it. I knew that if I wanted to make something of myself, I had to keep working toward that college degree. When most of my friends graduated after four years of college, I realized that I was still two years away from receiving my degree. While I wished I could have been at the same point in my life as they were in theirs, I knew I would be there soon.

It takes everyone a different amount of time and usually a different number of steps to reach their personal goals and dreams. I had a college acquaintance ask me after my first four years if I was still planning on pursuing the whole "college thing." I quickly responded that I was not going to get this far just to suddenly turn around and quit. There were certainly times that school looked as if it would never end, but I did it. I have many wonderful memories of great professors and classes taken during my college years. I also have many memories of professors not understanding that I was physically in a wheelchair, but intellectually I was just like all of my fellow peers. I learned a lot about myself in dealing with those professors. My determination and desire to graduate came in handy when dealing with a difficult professor because of his or her misperceptions about me. I know that besides gaining an abundance of information while at college, I matured into a much more confident person. Becoming more aware of ourselves is part of the college experience, and I am glad I was able to work hard enough to see it develop. The bottom line is that something easy to attain is not always as satisfying as reaching dreams or goals that take rigorous work.

Because of that rigorous work I put in, graduating from college was an incredible feeling of accomplishment. So, to celebrate, I had a surprise up my little sleeve for my family and friends. As the president of Augustana College called "Kendra Elizabeth Gottsleben," I enthusiastically hopped out of my wheelchair and walked across the stage to receive my diploma. It will be another day in my life I shall never forget for as long as I live. I can truly say that, at this point in my life, there is nothing that can compare to the feeling of walking across that stage and receiving my college diploma after working toward it for six years.

Pushing Myself to Achieve New Goals

Writing also takes a lot of determination within oneself. Even though I had never thought writing a book seemed impossible (because I take great pleasure in writing), it is still a time-consuming process. My goal of writing a book was only to be able to say I wrote a book and share my experiences in life to show how I have overcome obstacles. My goal has never been to become famous or make tons of money from it. I simply took on the challenge of writing a book to prove to myself I could accomplish it and hopefully help others along the way. I am tremendously proud of my ability to write. Many people have shown great interest in my book, and their enthusiasm has contributed to my motivation. Sometimes it helps when more people than just yourself are pushing you to achieve a goal. I also realized quickly that I had to give myself deadlines to be successful in producing the final product. My deadline for the first draft was the end of the summer of 2010. My next goal was to find an editor and publisher or decide to self-publish. After deciding to self-publish, I was able to connect with a friend and fellow Augustana graduate to help me edit the book. Since then, there have been many other steps to the process, including finding the right company to help me print my book, finding a photographer to take photos for the front and back cover of my book, and ultimately deciding whether I should start a business based off of my book and its mission. Being as strong-minded as I am I always knew that I could complete a book once I sat down and started to actually write. While it hasn't been easy by any means, it has been a goal I've thoroughly enjoyed pursuing.

I have always had high expectations of myself, and I know that many others in society also have the same type of expectations of themselves. Sadly, as a society, there are people who have a tendency to sell others and themselves short, no matter what their circumstances in life may be. Countless people have been told that they are never going to be able to reach their ambitions. When I think about these types of situations, I get extremely disappointed because many people take what others say to heart no matter how false it might be. People are always going to give their input to others, even when it is not asked for. I believe that if people truly try their best and never give up on themselves, then they can accomplish absolutely anything they want to accomplish. Of course, it does not mean those dreams and goals will be achieved without any obstacles. As I have stated before, we as individuals need to recognize that we are the ones who determine what our future holds for us, not anyone else.

Inspiring Determination: The Hoyt Family

A perfect example of determination can be found in a great father-son pair, Dick and Rick Hoyt. These two demonstrate that, even with a physical disability, they can be just as successful at achieving a goal as anyone else can be. Dick Hoyt, the father, and Rick Hoyt, the son, work together as a team to accomplish Rick's dream. Rick had a dream of running a marathon. The challenge was that, as a result of a lack of oxygen to Rick's brain at the time of his birth, he was diagnosed as a spastic quadriplegic with cerebral palsy. Dick and his wife Judy were informed that institutionalizing Rick was the best thing for him because there was no chance of Rick recovering. The parents were also told that there was little hope for Rick to ever live a "normal" life. But as parents they soon realized that Rick was able to learn and understand just like everyone else. Once Dick and Judy found a certain type of computer that could assist him in communicating with others, Rick was able to use his voice to talk for himself, just like most people in society do.

One day Rick told his father that he wanted to take part in a five-mile benefit run for a Lacrosse player who had an accident that resulted in the player becoming paralyzed. Dick agreed to push Rick in his wheelchair even though Dick had never been a long-distance runner. This was the first run of many for "Team Hoyt." While it was Rick's first chance at reaching his goal of running a marathon, it certainly would not be his last. One time, Rick told his father that when he is running he feels like he is not disabled. Someone once asked Rick if he could do anything for his father what it would be. Rick quickly answered that he would like to have his father sit in the wheelchair and he would push his father for once.

It is apparent while watching Rick Hoyt in his wheelchair that he has had huge physical obstacles throughout his life. With help from his father, Rick is able to compete in events that many people *without* disabilities cannot even imagine doing. Also, despite his physical disability, Rick has gone through the public school system and graduated from college. There are many people in this country that have no physical obstacles whatsoever who have not attended college, simply because they do not believe that they can accomplish it.

I was fortunate enough to hear Dick Hoyt speak at a banquet a few years ago, and what I remember is Dick saying that people think that, as a father, all he has gotten out of running is seeing his son happy. He told the audience that is not the only thing that has come from their teamwork. Dick said when he and Rick are running together, it is their time to forget about the world around them and just feel the freedom that comes with running. I think that's a fantastic thing to think about. Sometimes the work we put into achieving our goals can lead to outcomes we would've never even imagined. For more info on the Hoyt family and their efforts, visit www.teamhoyt.com.

Making the Most of Life

Personally, I have always had the mindset of never wasting a day that I have been given here on Earth. God gives us gifts each and every day; we just have to be open to receiving them in any way, shape or form they come. Each morning I make the decision that whatever occurs during that particular day, no matter how it could potentially be a challenge or set me back as I pursue my goals, I will not let it deter me. I am also determined to show others that they have no need to ever feel remorseful or apologetic toward me. It is a waste of their time. I am an enormously blessed person. When I look at my life I see that if I did not have Mucopolysaccharidosis Type VI, I would not be the person I am today. Even though there have been some definite challenges that I have had to overcome in life, I also see that without those obstacles I would not have many other wonderful memories, such as sitting in box seating at a San Francisco Giants baseball game, traveling to Vancouver, BC, as a speaker on a patient advisory board, being a part of medical research trial or meeting other MPS individuals and their families. I believe in God's plan for who comes into our lives and what we get to experience in life. With every difficulty during life there are always benefits that we must be open to as positive experiences. If you are not open to possibilities you may end up limiting your life achievements.

Chapter 14

"A day without laughter is a day wasted."
-Charlie Chaplin

Lending a Helping Hand

My Personal Philosophy

Many people in our world have a philosophy that directs their lives each and every day. My philosophy in life is to lend a hand to others before asking for help myself. Beyond simply being a philosophy, helping others has become a lifestyle choice for me. The feeling of happiness I receive when I assist a friend, family member, co-worker, or even a stranger is what keeps me motivated to live life to the fullest. I prefer to avoid individuals who only offer to help someone knowing they will want or need something from that person down the road. These people assist others knowing that they themselves will benefit from the process. They do things for others with the mindset of "I'll scratch your back if you scratch mine," which will not get them very far in life. The people who actually make a difference and achieve their greatest potential help others from the goodness of their hearts with no hidden agenda.

A few years ago, a friend of mine asked me to design posters for his jewelry company. I did not hesitate in volunteering my creative skills and ability on the computer so that he could promote his business. In my opinion, that is what friends do for each other. Just because I did the work on a volunteer basis does not mean I didn't get anything out of it. What I got was the realization that my creative eye does not only have to be just a hobby, but could be a way of making a career for myself one day. I am a person who wants to see other people accomplish something they have always dreamed of doing in their lifetime. If I can be of assistance in any way shape or fashion, then I will do what I can.

Using My Experiences to Give Back

Another way of helping that gives me happiness is when I am asked to speak at conferences and similar events. These conferences are places where I am asked to inform others about issues dealing with having a disability or, specifically, having MPS VI. A few years ago, I traveled to Mount Marty College in Yankton, South Dakota, to talk to their faculty about what it is like to be a student with a disability in a college setting. I was told that the college was new to the idea of having disability services. I enjoyed lending a hand to Mount Marty College, because I want professors to understand that even though an individual might have a disability, it doesn't mean they do not have the same aspirations and abilities as a student without a disability. I explained that it does not matter if someone has a learning disability or has a physical disability, they want to be treated the same as everyone else. Because having disability services on their campus was sort of a new idea, I explained how I received accommodations while attending Augustana College. I also went on to discuss how the responsibilities for providing accommodations are pretty standard for all colleges when it comes to supporting students with disabilities.

Besides speaking about living with disabilities in general, I also had the opportunity to speak at conferences dealing with the issues of MPS VI for three summers in a row. I attended the Patient Advisory Board Meeting in Vancouver BC, in 2008, in San Francisco, California, in 2009, and in Minneapolis, Minnesota, in 2010. At all three meetings, I spoke with other individuals with MPS VI about how we handle our lives. We talked about managing school classes and homework with weekly infusions, dealing with doctor appointments and insurance issues, obtaining employment, and how to stay up-to-date on our health condition.

I also had the privilege to travel to Aberdeen, South Dakota, to be a mentor at the Youth Leadership Forum (YLF) camp. This camp is designed to enable young adults with disabilities to learn from each other and also learn from successful adults with disabilities who are recognized leaders and role models. Students learn about their own disability as well as others' disabilities while learning to analyze their strengths and weaknesses and learn how to make good decisions. They also discover the importance of organizational skills, are introduced to different leadership styles, hear about the legislative process and disability laws, and gain insight into how to best influence others. Most importantly they begin to see that they must be their own advocates.

I had an amazing time helping the students learn to become more confident with their disability and know that they are not alone. It was also great to see them learn that we are the only ones who ultimately determine the attitude and approach we take in life. After sharing my own story, I had several students come up to me and ask more questions about how I overcame my struggles. I even had a few kids say, "Thank you for sharing...you really have helped me!" Also when the parents came to pick up their child, I had a mother come over to me saying she was so happy that I was her child's mentor because her daughter was impressed with what I have accomplished despite my obstacles. Her daughter even gave me a hug thanking me before she left. I had no idea that I had even made an impact on her, let alone an impact worth such a strong display of gratitude.

In my opinion, there are few better feelings than having a teenager or teenagers come and thank me for what I have shared with them about my life. One of my goals in life has always been to help others with their disabilities or medical conditions, and I feel blessed that I am able to do that for people. There were so many moments throughout that week when I observed the young adults lighting up with the confidence to not give up on themselves just because they have a disability. They learned to never give up on their dreams and goals in life. Needless to say, I am hoping that I will be asked to continue mentoring students at the Youth Leadership Forum in future years.

Numerous times people have told me that my outlook on life is incredible with all that I have had to deal with. The real truth is I know that there are others in this world who have had worse life circumstances than me. I have grown to appreciate my life challenges, because they have helped me become a better person and have helped me develop empathy for others. If I can improve someone else's life for a minute or two, then I experience a sense of success. The great feeling of fulfillment I gain as I try to help others who live with MPS VI (or any other hurdle) motivates me to keep up my efforts no matter what it takes. I know that when I was diagnosed, there was not much information about MPS VI. I want to be able to inspire families in realizing that anything is possible. It may be a long road to reach their goals in life, but the road is worth it when the goals are accomplished. Look at me! I am a prime example, as a college graduate with a liberal arts degree who double majored in sociology and psychology.

Helping Strangers (and Helpful Strangers)

Recently I had a father from India contact me through Facebook asking if I could give advice to him and his wife on how to help their nine month old son, recently diagnosed with MPS Type VI, to live a "normal" life. We talked about the enzyme treatment drug and he said that it cannot be imported to India as of now. There are many rules and regulations that are very different in other countries regarding drug treatments. I told him I would help him in any way that I could and I sent him a link to a speech I did for TEDxSiouxFalls, which is an event meant to share and spread important ideas. I wanted him to hear my speech because it talked about living with MPS VI and making the most of my life even in the face of adversity. The father responded, "Hi Kendra! This is so inspiring and heartening. Thanks for the wonderful video and heartfelt appreciation and wishes for the wonderful goals you have set for yourself. I really appreciate your parents as well because I know that as parents what it takes to have a child with such a rare genetic disorder and it has all been but only 4 months in my case....I have also sent you a friend request as it would be my pleasure to have you as my guiding force for treating & bringing up my little baby." I have been honored to continue to assist these parents. Whether I'm speaking with people who live with a disability or a medical condition such as MPS, those people's families, or anyone in general, my main objective is to communicate that we all may look different on the exterior but, at the same time, we can be similar on the inside. We all need to understand that, as long as we all have a passion for giving back to others and we stay true to ourselves, we can accomplish greatness. We are all God's creatures, and He wants us to be kind to one another. God rallies around us, so let us rally around His creatures whenever one needs assistance.

Throughout my life I have had many encounters with strangers who have given me an item for no apparent reason. I have had strangers approach me to hand me bracelets, stuffed animals, tree ornaments, arrowheads, carvings and the list goes on. These people came quickly into my life and left just as quickly. Even with their short presence, they made an everlasting impact on my life. These people gave me the item from the goodness of their hearts expecting nothing back from me, but perhaps a wide smile of gratitude.

One example of this took place at the restaurant called "Grandmas" in Minneapolis, Minnesota. This restaurant was across the street from the hotel my parents and I were staying at prior to a surgery I was going to have a couple of days later. Our waitress was personable and friendly to my parents and me throughout our dinner. She asked us what brought us to Minneapolis and my father responded that I was going to be having a surgery in a couple of days at the University of Minnesota Medical Center. She was so considerate of my feelings that she bent down to my level at the table and asked if she could give me something, and I said sure. She asked me to put my wrist out and then placed a leather-braided friendship bracelet around it. As she was doing so, the waitress explained that the bracelet was her "lucky bracelet" and how it had worked for her numerous times throughout her life, and now she wanted to pass on her luck to me for my surgery. I thanked her and smiled and said she was very kind to give me her "lucky bracelet." I was young at the time and was not as astonished at what she had given me as my parents were. I very much appreciated her generosity, but at that time I was more preoccupied and concerned about the upcoming surgery that was to follow.

Many years later I have realized how thoughtful that waitress was in giving me her bracelet. She was giving straight from her heart to another individual whom she had never met before and probably would never see again. She easily could have just said that she was sorry about my situation rather than giving me something so special and dear to her, but she did not. This waitress gave me her "lucky bracelet" because she was selfless and wanted to share luck with me. She was one of the first strangers in my life to give me an item for no apparent reason.

Another time I was eating in Red Lobster with my father and my Gottsleben grandparents when a fellow who looked like he could have been someone's grandpa came over to our table and asked my father if he could give me something he had carved. My father was hesitant, but decided that the guy seemed pleasant enough. What he gave me was a carving shaped as a bird with Tweety Bird's face painted on it. He informed us that he made these carvings to pass out to people whom he considered to be special individuals. I was surprised to see how much work this man did to make sure that the people he thought were special knew they were. This person's dedication toward others made an impression on me, even at fourteen. He had an actual purpose in creating the Tweety Bird carvings. This man's actions led me to believe he was someone who throughout his life showed others they were unique and special.

This man's Tweety Bird carving was another thoughtful incident that has taken place in my life, which shows goodhearted people are out there in our world. But I do have to be honest. When he came over to our table, I was also hesitant, like my father, because I did not know what he wanted to give me. Sadly, many of us have the initial reaction of hesitation when strangers approach us. We have been trained to be cautious with people we do not know because something dreadful could happen. But what really needs to happen is that we become more open to others, because we never know how other people can influence our lives. As I have grown, I have been somewhere in between these two mindsets of caution and openness. Receiving these gifts throughout my life has contributed to my openness towards others. When people open themselves to others, *that* is when humans have the chance to receive greatness from others.

I have had many encounters with strangers who give, but I want to share one more example. My mother and I met a lady sitting in the Denver, Colorado, airport while we were waiting for our plane to Oakland, California. The woman and my mother were discussing why each was traveling to Oakland. As they were talking I noticed that the lady had a beautiful ankle bracelet on, and I complimented her on it. She laughed and commented to us that she thought she was probably too old to be wearing an ankle bracelet since she was a grandma. I grinned and told her there was no age limit on ankle bracelets. I told her that she did not appear to be that old, so she had to have been a younger grandma. The lady thanked me for the compliment, and we all three went about our conversation. As we boarded the plane, we went our separate ways to our seats and settled in. A good hour of traveling went by with me sleeping most of the time and my mother dozing off and on. When I awoke my mother handed me the ankle bracelet I had noticed the woman wearing earlier. My expression must have been a look of puzzlement, because she laughed at me and told me I was seeing straight. My mother explained that while I was sleeping, she had felt a tap on her shoulder, and it was the lady we had talked to earlier in the airport. My mother went on to say that the lady wanted me to have the ankle bracelet because I had liked it so much, and I was a younger woman who could get more use out of it. I could not believe my eyes and decided to put it on right away. When we were unloading from the plane, I saw her pass by and quickly thanked her and said she had not needed to give her ankle bracelet to me. She smiled and remarked that she knew she did not have to, but she wanted to.

This woman had no real specific reason to give me her ankle bracelet other than the fact that we made a real connection. As a result of my mother and I being truly open and honest about ourselves, she was invited to be open and honest with us about herself. In today's world there are too many people out there that give something to someone and later are expecting something in return. We as a society are not used to stumbling upon a person who gives just to give or to make someone smile. We all like to be appreciated by others, so we need to try to not be suspicious when a wonderful person actually does appreciate us simply for who we are. Seeing life with this mindset is something we all can work on.

Over the years I have been an extremely fortunate person for all the wonderful individuals who have come into my life, no matter the extent of time I have been able to spend with them. Everyone we interact with makes an imprint on our lives— regardless of who they are—if we just let them. We all have interactions with others that may be wonderful and exciting or unpleasant and displeasing, but we learn from every experience. I believe life is all about helping and giving to others with no anticipation of receiving something back. I believe that hearing the words "thank you" is always appreciated, but the bottom line is if you are helping or giving to someone in hopes of receiving something back, then the generosity is not truly heartfelt and can sometimes be lost because of the motives. So in my opinion, it really is true in life that the more you give, the more you get. As you live your life, keep in mind that one of the best ways to have a positive impact on the world is to give. You never know whose life you'll change when you give selflessly.

A Special Angel

I was prepared for surgery by
the attentive doctors and nurses around me.
Thoughts of Julie kept me calm,
knowing she was present gave me Faith.

Safe and protected in the doctor's hands, and
my mom by my side, I gave my concerns to God.
As I looked at the bright lights above me, my eyes became heavy,
the time had come for me to close my eyes and trust.

After I awoke, I would learn that the surgery didn't work out as
intended, but the doctor's split second decision kept me alive.
I coded twice on the OR table and no one knows how I am laying
here talking, explaining to the doctors I said, "You had a little
help from a friend of mine, her name is Julie and she
is my Guardian Angel."

Faith and trust are powerful beliefs…and so are Special Angels.

Written in high school

Chapter 15

*"Every great dream begins with a dreamer.
Always remember, you have within you
the strength, the patience, and the passion
to reach for the stars to change the world."*
—Harriet Tubman

Starting a Movement

The First Step

As a 27-year-old, I realize that I still have much more of my life to look forward to and live before I can ever say that I have fulfilled God's plan for me here on Earth. I have much more to experience as I discover what He has in store for me. I also have dreams and goals that I have yet to reach, and nothing is going to stop me from accomplishing them – that much I know for sure. One such aspiration is to someday start a movement committed to reaching out to all kinds of people who may be struggling with life's challenges, and I would love for this book to be a catalyst for that movement. I am passionate about this idea because I truly believe that, no matter who we are, we all have struggled at some time or another in life. Everyone in society needs to recognize that those struggles and challenges make us stronger within ourselves, both now and in the future.

Speaking to others about achieving triumphs despite life's obstacles is something I greatly enjoy doing. I especially love to reach out to children and young adults who have to face physical or learning challenges and help them understand that there is a way to overcome bullying, that they can achieve great success, and that they should never give up on themselves. I am also very passionate about talking with parents of children who have life-threatening illnesses or disabilities, simply to educate those parents on how I was raised and how they can encourage their children to attend college, graduate school, or even receive their doctorate if that is such a goal. In addition, I want parents to see that encouraging their children to become independent individuals is achievable.

Having the ability to assist others with their journey of self-confidence and success is one way I know I can give back. It is a way of demonstrating to everyone that daring to dream is healthy for an individual's attitude, and that we should never stop pushing toward the future. That mindset generates a sense of knowledge that we are always changing for the better. When people stop dreaming for their future, they lose sight of all that they one day wish to accomplish. As someone with experience in facing obstacles, I consider my purpose on Earth to be showing others that, even with the obstacles we are given, we can still achieve greatness.

Becoming Who I Am Today

I have been through many difficult circumstances during life that have led me to where I am today. I completely acknowledge that without those tough times I would not have been able to become the person I am now. For every hurdle, a positive effect follows once the hurdle has been cleared. Given some time, that positive outcome will become clear to you. The message I want to pass on is that one's attitude toward life affects the outcomes that occur throughout it. It does not matter if someone has physical challenges, learning challenges, or some other type of life obstacle; life can still be fulfilling, despite those hardships. I have lived with that type of mindset since I was a young child. I know that my optimism is why I am able to say that my life up to this point has been as great as I have worked to make it.

Negativity is very damaging to one's life and will never get anyone very far. I have seen a few people with disabilities who have given up on pursuing college or looking forward to their future beyond high school. I am always heartbroken when I hear about a person who has given up on his or her future. The outlook on life I like is positivity, because the more you see positivity in situations, the more open you will be to possibilities that can later end in overwhelming success. Being positive is a part of who I am, and I make that choice each day, even on the days when it would have been much easier not to be optimistic. I see a glass and say it is half full and not half empty. I have lived my life with the attitude that I am just like everyone else on the inside, despite some different height levels and physical characteristics on the outside. I have had to learn to deal with the awkwardness of being so short while talking with others who are standing. I recognize my short stature as a unique characteristic of being me, and, because I cannot change it, I do not dwell on it. We all have our unique characteristics that we need to own and appreciate. I would love for you to take time each day and recognize your unique characteristics and be proud of them, because God cares greatly for you and chose those characteristics just for you. The sooner we do that, the sooner we will be confident in achieving our goals and dreams. Everyone should be respected and loved in the world, no matter what their unique characteristics are.

Taking the Journey

Everyone's life is a journey. Some journeys are filled with more challenges and obstacles than others. The paths our lives travel help us form our own personal ideas of what we feel we can or cannot achieve and accomplish. Of course, some of those notions about ourselves—like our beliefs that we may not be able to achieve our dreams or goals—are not always entirely true.

Many people need to understand that we all must at least *try* to make steps toward our ambitions before we disregard our hopes for success. And yes, sometimes failure is an outcome that occurs when working toward achieving those accomplishments, but that does not mean we should stop believing in ourselves. Because for every door that closes, another one opens up (I know it's cliché, but it really is true). And believe me, they do open. Maybe not in the exact way we may think though, which is why we have to be open-minded. If you ponder about successful people, you are reminded that there are not many people in society who can say they have found instant success. There are a select few people who have actually made it big with immediate success, but realistically it takes many attempts and failures in the process before someone triumphs in success. We all have different ways of reaching our ambitions. The bottom line is that accomplishing our dreams and goals all comes down to determination. There is no right or wrong way of achieving those goals or dreams for ourselves. Being patient, diligent, and never giving up on ourselves are the most important factors in achieving all that we hope to during life.

One area in which I plan to find my own sense of success is reaching out to and encouraging those who may be struggling with challenges and obstacles. We all need an individual in our lives that helps encourage and motivate us to become the person we have always wanted to be. We all need to realize that reaching our dreams is achievable – all we need is persistence.

Words of Wisdom

I have had many people in my lifetime give me pieces of advice on all aspects of life, even when I have not asked for advice. But with all of the great advice I have received over the years, the most important has been to be true to myself, surround myself with people who wholeheartedly believe in me, and never give up even when life gets rough. These pieces of advice are probably not that surprising after reading much of my book, because those comments have greatly guided much of my attitude. I learned at a young age that the only one who defines who we are is ourselves. The only thing in life we can control is ourselves and the way we react to our circumstances and environment. Staying true to who we are is what will make us successful regardless of how grand our ambitions may be. Changing our opinions or values for someone else is harmful because that is when we lose ourselves. Then we do not know whether we are trying to achieve a goal because *we* want to or because someone else wants us to. I have stayed true to who I am by acknowledging my personal limitations and also by recognizing what I have to offer others, such as optimism, laughter, and empathy, and I strongly encourage others I know to always stay true to who they are.

This leads to the next piece of advice, which is being around others who *do* believe in what we can do, rather than being around people who point out what we *cannot* do. It is never healthy to be around others who always put you down. We all run into people like this in society, and I take what comes out of their mouths with a grain of salt. However, I do not always disregard everything others say; usually I analyze their words to see if there is something I can learn from that unsupportive person. But as a person who wants to make something of myself, I try to make connections with others who want to do the same within their own lives. Having people that surround you with positivity and support is great because when you come upon a hurdle, they are there for support when you need it.

The last piece of advice I want to share is the importance of never giving up on yourself. This is probably the most important one for me because of my life obstacles. I have faced numerous challenges, but have made the decision to not give up on myself when it comes to achieving my ambitions. Why? Because my limitations do not define who I am. I work hard to accomplish all my aims in life and show others that I do not just talk the talk, but also walk the walk (or roll the roll in my wheelchair) when it comes to achieving my goals. Writing a book was a goal for my life, and what you are holding in your hands is proof of my determination to reach that goal.

Success, and My Future

The secrets to my success have been not letting my Mucopolysaccharidosis, my being in a wheelchair, or my height interfere with all my ambitions. I am truthful with myself about my physical limitations and capabilities, realizing certain aims are achievable, but not without a lot of diligent work and self-motivation. I am able to realistically determine which goals and dreams are attainable given my resources and physical situation. I have been told that realistic people do not make it very far when talking about aspiring to write a book or become a public speaker, and I agree with that remark to a certain degree, because many people who have realistic attitudes are unable to think outside the box of possibilities. But I consider myself in between realism and a dreamer. If I were too realistic I would not have the guts to put myself out there with this book or speaking engagements. I am a little bit like Don Quixote, in that I will attack the windmills in my life, but I also understand Sancho Panza who waits around to pick up the pieces. I am fond of sharing my experiences of bliss, struggles, and challenges with others so that they can learn from me to never give up their goals and dreams in life. When I share my stories, I in return learn from individuals about their own stories. I hope after reading this book people walk away with my message that we as humans should never let those obstacles deter us from pressing on to the next part of life and making the most of this life we've been given. That's what making lemonade from lemons is all about!

<u>Questions</u>

Where will I be in five years?

Will I have a fulfilling career with
remarkable individuals?

Will I be in a thoughtful and loving
relationship with a fantastic guy?

Will I have gone back to get
my Master's Degree?

Will I have assisted others within
the disability community?

Will I have started a small designing
business with my aunt?

Where will I be in ten years?

Will I have accomplished the goal of
working with children in a hospital setting?

Will I be married to an incredible man
that makes me laugh?

Will I have accomplished my goal
of writing a book?

Will I have traveled to all the amazing
places I have always wanted to go?

Will I have helped out with other medical
findings on Mucopolysaccharidosis treatments?

Who knows where I will be at any given point in my life.
As long as I keep placing my trust and faith in God,
I know everything will work out according to His plan.

Written April 2009

Epilogue

As I sit here and contemplate where I am now compared to where I was when I first began writing, I'm filled with excitement. Why? Because I've crossed off of my list yet another one of my numerous dreams in life. I began writing as an Augustana College senior while looking toward the future with high hopes of finding my place out in the "real world." And it was at that point that the next journey of my life began – finding a job where I could use my passion and experience to help others.

My dream was that I would someday work within an organization or hospital that helped children and their families who were battling life threatening illnesses or living with disabilities. As I had expected, I ran into roadblocks, but those only made me stronger and more persistent! It was challenging because I encountered a number of potential employers who had no flexibility when it came to the positions they were seeking to fill. These people were very black-and-white as far as trying to see how I could fit into their organizations. I was an applicant that looked great on paper, but when they saw me, they only saw that I was forty inches tall and in a wheelchair; they had no ability to envision what I could do for them beyond my limitations. To be honest, there were even a few times I heard the comment, "Oh, you're in a wheelchair? Maybe this position won't work for you then." But I didn't let that stop me from pushing forward through job interviews. I knew all I needed to do was to find an employer who saw that I could fill a niche, and could see how my talents would contribute to their organization.

I am extremely proud to say that, in November of 2010, I began working at the Center for Disabilities within the Sanford School of Medicine at the University of South Dakota. I know how fortunate and blessed I am to have been able to find a job so quickly after graduating from college, when so many college graduates are having a difficult time. I am excited to share with you that I could not have asked for any greater place to begin my career in helping others. Everyone I work with is positive and encouraging, and they see me as just another fellow employee despite our physical differences. It has truly been a dream come true for me. Sometimes, as I sit in my office, I still cannot believe how lucky I am. My boss, Judy, is the exact type of employer who I was hoping to find while job searching. She saw me, had an open mind about where I might fit in, and saw that I did, in fact, fill a niche. During our interview, Judy even remarked that she could see exactly how my talents could go beyond my position and ultimately contribute to the Center for Disabilities as a whole.

Oh, and I feel compelled to share the organization's mission statement – "Dedicated to Life Without Limits." Could there be a mission statement any more fitting for someone like me? I mean seriously, I have lived much of my life with the attitude that no one, not even myself, can put limits on me; to say that I am now working for an organization that believes the same is pretty darn incredible. This is a prime example that God has had a plan for me; I just have to keep believing and trusting in Him. I feel as though I am also on the road toward being able to spread my message of hope and perseverance to others, encouraging people not to give up on themselves no matter what life might throw at them.

Another wonderful opportunity I was able to be a part of since finishing my book was that I had the honor and pleasure of speaking at the first ever *TedxSiouxFalls* event. According to its website, TEDx is an independently organized event in the spirit of ideas worth spreading. At a TEDx event, live speakers and TED Talks videos combine to spark deep discussion and connection in a small group. The TED Conference provides general guidance for the TEDx program, but individual TEDx events are self-organized. I was asked to speak by the person organizing the event. We made a connection through Twitter, and I was told that my name was given by Jolene Loetscher, a fellow TEDx speaker. Jolene had shared that she thought I had an amazing story of overcoming obstacles in life and that my story needed to be shared.

When discussing the TEDx event, I was told that I could talk about whatever I felt I needed to share about my journey thus far. As we talked, I knew right away that I was going to talk about overcoming all of the obstacles and challenges I have had to deal with throughout my life, from elementary school all the way up to trying to find a career I was truly passionate about.

As the big day neared, I began to get more and more nervous. Those million butterflies I mentioned before in Chapter 9 were starting to flutter back. But along with the butterflies, I also felt a lot of excitement in being on stage for the first time in front of a 100-person audience. I knew that the feeling of accomplishment was going to feel absolutely amazing after I finished...and, just like I expected, it did feel amazing! I was fortunate enough to have my parents, Grandma Drew and two of my aunts in the audience. I was ecstatic that they were all there to share in my moment, as I set out to do something I have always wanted to do. Sharing my story has always been a long-time dream of mine, despite my nerves. But I have been told countless times that if someone did not get nervous it would mean that the passion from their talk was gone. My passion will never be gone!

I was and still am grateful for Jolene suggesting my name. The TEDx event gave me my first avenue to share my story, and it can now be seen by anyone who types in my name. Jolene led me to the realization that my dream of sharing my story is definitely something I should be doing. Her support and confidence in me has created a feeling of "Let's go Kendra, the world is ready for you!" If you'd like to see my TEDx talk, just visit *TEDxSiouxFalls.com* and look for my name under the "Speakers" section.

As I end this book, I want to leave you with my favorite quote, which I have already mentioned a few times throughout the book: "When life hands you lemons, make lemonade," or my extra special twist to the phrase: "When life hands you lemons, turn right around and squeeze those lemons to make the *BEST* lemonade possible!"

I live my life by this motto, and I hope this book has inspired you to live your life by that motto too.

Acknowledgements

Writing a book does not come easy, or without help from countless others. I have been tremendously fortunate for the many individuals who have assisted me in ideas, topics, editing, motivation, and support throughout the whole process of writing this book. I would like to take the time to thank the individuals who have taken time out of their busy lives and schedules to help me pursue my own dream of writing this book. I could not have done any of this without each of you. Every one of these individuals has played a large part in my life. Thank you so much! I greatly appreciate all that you have done for me.

Mary Barse – I have been incredibly blessed to have an aunt like you who has helped me with editing my chapters from the get go and giving ideas when I got stuck. When you found out I was going to write a book you were the first one telling me if I ever needed any help on any of the editing, you would be there to assist. It was a great motivator to see the enthusiasm and confidence you had for me taking on the task of writing a book.

Mike Billeter – Your diligent work with me to make this book the best it could be, all the way down to the last detail, is something I will forever be grateful to you for. I know that without your help and support I would probably still be in the "looking for an editor process" rather than having others reading the final product. I always enjoyed checking my e-mail to see what you had come up with for me to make my book better. I would love to work with you again on other book projects in the future!

Jenny Chavers – I asked you to write the foreword of this book because you have known me since I was a little baby and have seen me grown into the person I am today. You have always been there to cheer me on, even coming back to South Dakota for both my high school and college graduations. It has been another one of God's blessings having you in my life. As I have grown older, we have been able to confide in each other—just like two sisters would—about life's joys and worries, and it has been wonderful.

Betsy Drew – God blessed me with you as a mother, friend, and editor. I have gained so much from you, from what you taught me as a young child to today, where I still learn from you every day. Thank you for helping me become the person I am today, despite the fact you will never take the credit you deserve. You never accepted the word "can't" which is why I have never limited myself. It is a privilege and honor to be able to call you my mother.

Cathy Drew – I am so happy with the work you did in designing the front and back cover of this book and the layout of the inserted pictures! When I first saw my title and name on the picture I chose for the front cover, it all began to feel real for me. It made me so excited to see your amazing work covering the words I had been working so hard on for the last few years. I knew you would be the perfect person as my cover designer with your creative eye, and you did an amazing job! Above and beyond what I could have imagined.

Dan Drew – The idea of owning my own business was a scary idea for me, but with your guidance in deciding what were the best steps to take gave me the strength and courage I needed to pursue this dream. I am so grateful to have received such reliable and sincere advice from you, especially when I needed it the most. Your unwavering confidence not only in my ability as a writer, but also in the success of my book, particularly when we discussed ways to get it distributed into stores, was remarkable. You were always telling me, "Kendra we can get that done! No problem!" I feel so blessed to have an uncle that was willing to guide me on this journey and that had faith in this huge project.

Jeanne Drew – I feel so fortunate for your endless and unwavering faith in me and my abilities throughout my life. Throughout all of my accomplishments, you have always been there cheering me on in the audience or waiting to congratulate me with a huge hug. I was so excited to give you a draft of my book to read and get your opinion, which I truly value. Upon reading the draft, you told me that you could not have been more proud to be my grandma, that was absolutely the best feedback I could receive and it gave me the strength I needed to continue with the process of achieving my dream of becoming a published author. I am so blessed to have you in my life!

Dave Gottsleben – As your daughter, the endlessness of support and love throughout my life has always encouraged me to reach for the stars and beyond. Overcoming life's hurdles is something that was normal to me as a child, no matter how challenging they were. I will never forget the day I told you about starting my own business and you so supportively offered to help by taking me to the courthouse to file the business papers. That was such a special moment to me and I am so thankful that I was able to start this dream with the support and love of my dad.

Helen Gottsleben – You have had the upmost confidence in my capabilities and dreams. I am so lucky to be able to call you my grandma. Everything I have achieved you have always been there telling me, "It's no surprise to me that you have reached you dreams, you are such a determined person!" It was so fun sharing the drafts of each chapter with you and hearing your input on each of them. I wholeheartedly valued the advice and suggestions you provided during the editing process; because of your thoughtful comments, I was able to develop your ideas to improve the book. We both have a passion for writing and we will forever have that in common. I am so proud to be a Gottsleben!

Sara Javers – As a photographer, you took my vision for what I wanted my book covers to look like and made it come true. You do amazing work, *that* is for sure. There was no one else I would have chosen but you for doing my front and back cover photos. From the first day I met you, I knew there was something incredible about you. We may look different, but at the same time we have had to take similar paths when it comes to hospitals. I am so honored that you were so eager to help me make my book as perfect on the outside as it is in the inside.

John Kreklow – You provided me with the extra push I needed to start this huge process of accomplishing my dream. Without your encouragement and inspiration, I may still be thinking about writing this book – and now I'm holding the finished product in my hands! The chapter outlines you suggested also gave me a great jumping off point to begin writing. Thank you for keeping tabs on my progress throughout each stage of the writing process; it was very helpful! Your friendship and supportive advice to never let a dream become unattainable have empowered me with the drive to accomplish this book and so much more.

Mitch Peterson – I am incredibly lucky to have had your help with advising me on the legal steps that I needed to take to make sure my book was a successful adventure for myself. I greatly appreciate you taking time out of your already busy caseload to answer my questions and concerns throughout the writing process. When I began thinking of all the legal things it took to successfully write a book, I started to feel overwhelmed and nervous, then after asking you my countless questions I began to feel at ease and confident.

Taylor Ptacek – I feel so blessed that, despite you being on your new adventure of becoming a lawyer, you still wanted to assist in editing some last minute changes of the book. For that, I am forever grateful. You are a special friend who never let even a few days go by without sharing some encouraging words of how proud you were of me with this book, which always made me smile. We have only known each other for a short period of time, but it feels as though we have known each other for a lifetime already!

Theresa Ring – I love how you wanted to help me edit my book while taking the time from your busy schedule in Tanzania, Africa as a member of the Peace Corps. You offering your assistance despite being a world away from me makes me feel extraordinarily blessed with your friendship and encouragement. Being able to share this experience with you is great because we have known each other since pre-school. A friend like you is why I have so many wonderful friend memories in life.

While I could probably write an entire book just about everyone who has come into my life through the years, I feel compelled to group you all. I am so sorry I cannot thank each and every one of you separately, but please know that I am honored to know you. The bottom line is that I could not have become the person I am today without each and every one of you being a part of my life. Thank you so very much and God bless!

References

Catholic Women's Devotional Bible: New Revised Standard Version. Grand Rapids, MI: Zondervan Pub. House, 2000. Print.

MPS Society. Web. 2011. 6 April 2009. <http://www.mpssociety.org/>.

Rogness, Alvin N. *Book of Comfort*. Minneapolis: Augsburg Pub. House, 1979. Print.

Team Hoyt. Web. 2011. 2 May 2010. <http://www.teamhoyt.com/index.html>.

Teen Study Bible. New International Version. Grand Rapids, MI: Zondervan, 2002. Print.

Meeks, Wayne A., and Jouette M. Bassler. *The HarperCollins Study Bible: New Revised Standard Version*. New York, NY: HarperCollins, 1993. Print.

"YLF." *TSLP*. Web. 25 August 2011. <http://www.tslp.org/YLF.htm>.

Pausch, Randy, and Jeffrey Zaslow. *The Last Lecture*. New York: Hyperion, 2008. Print.

Warren, Rick. *The Purpose Driven Life*. Grand Rapids, MI: Zondervan, 2002. Print.